Ultimate EKG Breakdown

Anthony H. Kashou, M.D.

Ultimate EKG Breakdown
FIRST EDITION

EKG.MD

The Premier EKG Resource for Medical Professionals.

Anthony H. Kashou, M.D.

Copyright © 2019 by The EKG Guy, Inc. Copying or distributing any content within this book without permission can result in serious legal action. 2019 EKG.MD. All rights reserved. This course is designed for educational purposes only and not to diagnose, treat, or offer medical advice.

EKG.MD
Ultimate EKG Breakdown

ISBN 978-1-7335581-0-5

Printed in the United States of America

Copyright © 2019 by The EKG Guy, Inc.

All rights reserved. No part of this publication may be reproduced, distributed, or transmitted in any form, or by any means, electronic or mechanical, including photocopying, recording, information storage and retrieval system, without prior permission in writing from the publisher (email: theekgguy@EKG.MD).

Disclaimer
Ultimate EKG Breakdown is intended to provide an overview of ECG principles. It is not intended to be a working guide to patient care, drug administration, or medical treatment. The medicine evolves constantly, and it is common for changes in practice to occur. The treating practitioner is solely responsible to determine what is in the best interest of the patient, what tre is most appropriate, and how best to implement treatment. The treating practitioner should base his or her decision on his or her own independent expertise and knowledge of the patie publisher and the author deny all liability for any injury, damage, or harm to people or property arising from or related to the material within this publication.

Additionally, although this publication has been carefully assembled and is accurate to the best of the author's knowledge, the author and publisher make absolutely no representat guarantees, express or implied, with respect to the completeness, currency, or accuracy of the contents of this publication. This publication is not intended to be, and should not be, us substitute for the advice of a physician or other licensed and qualified medical professional. Some information included in this publication may refer to drugs, techniques, or devices, wh subject to government regulation, and it is the responsibility of the treating practitioner to comply with all relevant laws.

Published by The EKG Guy, Inc.
https://www.EKG.MD
theekggguy@EKG.MD

To my wife Brooke, daughter Vanessa, parents, and siblings for their endless love and support. Without them, none of this would be possible.

Dr. Anthony Kashou (The EKG Guy) is a physician resident at the Mayo Clinic in Rochester, Minnesota. He has taught developed curriculum for medical students, including 500+ lectures and 100+ hours of adult and pediatric ECG lessons. A Mayo Clinic, he pursues innovative ECG research and was awarded first place for his research at the Minnesota Amer College of Cardiology Conference 2018. His passion for medical education and innovation led to the developmen EKG.MD, which provides a convenient and accessible forum to learn the fundamentals and foundations of ECG interpreta He has also authored dozens of peer-reviewed articles for medical journals and textbooks.

Dr. Kashou continues to lead and teach weekly ECG sessions and weekend seminars for students, residents, nurses, technicians, and physician assistants at the Mayo Clinic. He has garnered an online following of over 300,000 individuals in than two years and is the founder of the largest, fastest growing ECG community in the world. His clinical research focuse developing innovative ECG algorithms that can be integrated and implemented into clinical practice.

Why This Resource Was Developed

...osting dozens of ECG sessions for nurses, ECG techs, residents, medical and nursing students, and other medical providers, one thing was clear: ...l professionals want better ECG learning options. ECG interpretation skills are critical for patient care, yet many providers feel unequipped to ...e even basic ECG proficiency. When I hosted an ECG education seminar, participants dramatically improved their ECG comprehension after only 5 ...of learning – proving even a small amount of time dedicated to learning ECGs can make a big difference! This resource helps medical providers ...ve their ability to make real-time medical decisions that will improve the quality and efficiency of patient care.

...ltimate EKG Breakdown is designed to fill a universal gap in the currently available options. Existing ECG resources tend to be either extremely basic ...advanced, with minimal clinical applicability. The Ultimate EKG Breakdown is designed to provide the most efficient way to learn about ECGs – ...from the beginner level and gradually progressing to an advanced interpreter level, focusing on clinical relevance and educational efficiency. My goal ...ake the most of your time, to give you practical educational tools, and to have a little fun while we're at it! And, if you want practice, don't worry – I've ...u covered. You can find an abundance of practice material at www.EKG.MD, along with daily ECG practice questions and hundreds of videos on ...KG Guy's Facebook page or YouTube channel – in fact, probably more practice material than you ever wanted.

...I started teaching ECGs, my goal was to provide every possible resource to help learners understand ECGs in the most efficient, helpful, and ...rehensive way in order to ultimately deliver better patient care. The Ultimate EKG Breakdown and all the additional resources developed are my ...t to do just that. I hope you enjoy this resource and will provide feedback to improve future versions. Always know you have a colleague here rooting ...u. Best of luck and remember to have fun!

Resource Benefits

Medical professionals who encounter ECGs in their clinical practice have three primary struggles that this course addresses:

1) They have busy work schedules and busy lives;
2) Patient care is compromised or delayed if the medical professional is not equipped to interpret ECGs; and
3) They often encounter ECGs that they feel unprepared to interpret.

Recognizing the busyness of medical professionals, the course is designed to be **efficient**.

- The course manual and lectures are designed to make efficient use of time and to provide a firm grasp of clinically relevant core concepts w wasting time. You can also choose to do only the High-Yield lectures recommended if you don't want a full ECG mastery.

To improve patient care, the course is **clinically relevant** and **comprehensive**.

- The course can take someone with no ECG knowledge all the way to the level of an advanced interpreter. You will benefit from cli applicable knowledge, regardless of whether you progress to a beginner, intermediate, or advanced interpreter level. Your book is supplem by lectures for EVERY topic to help aid in comprehension of the material and to add new pearls mentioned within them.

- The course will not only fill you with basic and advanced adult ECG topics, but you also have a chance to learn about congenital heart di and some of the accompanying ECG changes. And, if you were wondering about practice, you get that too! Practice is the key to mas anything, and the same holds true for mastering ECGs.

Finally, the course is **flexible**.

- The course is useful for a wide range of medical professionals and allows you to achieve as high a level of competence as you desire. Yo choose to progress to a beginner, intermediate, or even an advanced level at your own pace. Taken at any level, this course will reduce the nu of situations in which a medical professional is unprepared to interpret an ECG. From a total beginner to an already advanced ECG interp almost any medical professional in a field where ECG literacy is an asset to patient care will benefit from this course.

How To Use This Book

course was developed to make ECG learning simple, efficient, and fun! Each topic within the book is covered single page, and each page is accompanied by a lecture. The lectures are progressively organized, and they begin the very basics - the earlier lessons will serve as your foundation as you progress through the course to more nced topics.

table of contents on the next few pages, you will find a number next to each topic. That number refers to the corresponding page number within this book, as well as to its accompanying lecture number. This should e it easy to transition between the book and the lectures. You will also notice a star (★) next to some topics. e are high-yield topics and can be a helpful reference for those of you who simply want to learn the "must-s." You can complete these 75 high-yield topics and lectures in just over 12 hours for a "rapid review" learning n.

le the majority of the topics already include detailed notes, you may want to take your own notes as you watch ectures - don't be afraid to get in there and mark up your book! You can also add to your notes as your vledge of the topics advances and you glean new information from other resources. Those of you who have the ket version will find this extremely helpful in the clinical setting.

ly believe this course represents ECG education at its best. If you take the time to engage to the fullest, you will ichly rewarded! Thank you for trusting me with your ECG learning needs. I wish you the best in your future er!

r colleague,
nony Kashou, M.D.
EKG Guy

EKG.MD

EKG.MD Ultimate EKG Breakdown Contents

Part I: The Basics
- ★ 1.0 Cardiac Anatomy & Circulation
- ★ 2.0 Electrical Conduction System of the Heart
- 3.0 Action Potential & Automaticity
- ★ 4.0 Vectors & Electrical Axis
- ★ 5.0 Electrodes
- ★ 6.0 Standard Leads
- 7.0 Right-sided Leads
- 8.0 Posterior Leads
- ★ 9.0 ECG Paper
- ★ 10.0 Standard 12-Lead ECG
- ★ 11.0 Localizing ECG Leads
- ★ 12.0 Basic Terms
- ★ 13.0 Cardiac Cycle & Complex Formation
- 14.0 P Wave
- 15.0 Ta Wave
- 16.0 PR Segment
- 17.0 PR Interval
- 18.0 QRS Complex
- 19.0 QRS Nomenclature
- 20.0 Intrinsicoid Deflection

- 21.0 ST Segment
- 22.0 T Wave
- 23.0 QT Interval
- 24.0 U Wave
- 25.0 TP Segment
- ★ 26.0 PP & RR Intervals
- ★ 27.0 Determining Regularity
- ★ 28.0 Determining Rate
- ★ 29.0 Determining Axis (Frontal Plane)
- ★ 30.0 Transitional Zone
- ★ 31.0 R Wave Progression

Part II: Rhythms
- 32.0 Approach to Rhythms

Sinus Rhythms
- ★ 33.0 Normal Sinus Rhythm
- ★ 34.0 Sinus Arrhythmia
- ★ 35.0 Sinus Bradycardia
- ★ 36.0 Sinus Tachycardia
- 37.0 Sinus Pause & Arrest
- 38.0 Sinoatrial Exit Block

Atrial Rhythms
- ★ 39.0 Premature Atrial Contraction
- 40.0 Ectopic Atrial Tachycardia
- ★ 41.0 Wandering Atrial Pacemaker
- ★ 42.0 Multifocal Atrial Tachycardia
- ★ 43.0 Atrial Flutter
- ★ 44.0 Atrial Fibrillation

AV Junctional & Nodal Rhythms
- ★ 45.0 Premature Junctional Contraction
- ★ 46.0 Junctional Escape Beat
- ★ 47.0 Junctional Escape Rhythm
- 48.0 Accelerated Junctional Rhythm
- 49.0 AV Nodal Reentrant Tachycardia
- ★ 50.0 Wolff-Parkinson-White (WPW) Syndrome
- 51.0 Lown-Ganong-Levine (LGL) Syndrome
- 52.0 AV Reentrant Tachycardia

Ventricular Rhythms
- ★ 53.0 Premature Ventricular Contraction
- ★ 54.0 Ventricular Escape Beat
- ★ 55.0 Ventricular Escape (Idioventricular) Rhythm

★ High-Yield Topic

KG.MD Ultimate EKG Breakdown Contents

Ventricular Rhythms (continued...)

★ 56.0 Accelerated Idioventricular Rhythm
57.0 Fusion & Capture Beats
58.0 Brugada's & Josephson's Signs
★ 59.0 Ventricular Tachycardia
60.0 Reentrant Ventricular Tachycardia
★ 61.0 Torsades de Pointes
★ 62.0 Ventricular Flutter
★ 63.0 Ventricular Fibrillation
★ 64.0 Asystole
★ 65.0 Pulseless Electrical Activity
★ 66.0 Pacemaker Rhythms

Part III: Chamber Enlargement

Atrial Enlargement

★ 67.0 Right Atrial Enlargement
★ 68.0 Left Atrial Enlargement
69.0 Biatrial Enlargement

★ High-Yield Topic

Ventricular Hypertrophy

70.0 Right Ventricular Hypertrophy
★ 71.0 Left Ventricular Hypertrophy
72.0 Biventricular Hypertrophy

Part IV: Conduction Defects

AV Blocks

★ 73.0 First-Degree AV Block
★ 74.0 Second-Degree AV Block Mobitz I (Wenckebach)
★ 75.0 Second-Degree AV Block Mobitz II
★ 76.0 Third-Degree (Complete) AV Block
77.0 AV Dissociation

Intraventricular Conduction Defects

★ 78.0 Right Bundle Branch Block
★ 79.0 Left Bundle Branch Block
80.0 Left Anterior Fascicular Block
81.0 Left Posterior Fascicular Block
82.0 Bifascicular Block
83.0 Nonspecific Intraventricular Conduction Delay

EKG.MD Ultimate EKG Breakdown Content

Part V: Myocardial Ischemia & Infarction

84.0 Ischemic Heart Disease
85.0 Acute Myocardial Infarction
86.0 ECG Classification of Ischemic Heart Disease
★ 87.0 ECG Basics in Myocardial Ischemia & Infarction
★ 88.0 ST-T Basics in Acute Myocardial Ischemia
★ 89.0 Injury Currents: Transmural vs. Subendocardial Ischemia
★ 90.0 ECG Progression in Acute Myocardial Ischemia
★ 91.0 ST Elevation & Depression in Acute Myocardia Ischemia
★ 92.0 T-Wave Changes in Acute Myocardial Ischemia
93.0 Wellen's Syndrome
94.0 de Winter's Sign
95.0 T-Wave Pseudonormalization
★ 96.0 Pathological Q- & R-Waves
★ 97.0 Coronary Artery Anatomy & Dominance
★ 98.0 Left Ventricular Anatomy & Vascular Supply
★ 99.0 Localizing Ischemia in STEMI
★ 100.0 Right Coronary Artery Occlusion
★ 101.0 Left Anterior Descending Artery Occlusion
★ 102.0 Left Circumflex Artery Occlusion
★ 103.0 Left Main Coronary Artery Occlusion

★ 104.0 Prinzmetal's (Variant) Angina
105.0 Conduction System Vascular Supply
106.0 Conduction Defects in Myocardial Ischemia & Infarction
107.0 Sgarbossa Criteria
108.0 Conduction Defects in Inferior Wall MI
109.0 Conduction Defects in Anterior Wall MI

Part VI: Drugs & Electrolytes

★ 110.0 Digoxin
111.0 Hypercalcemia
112.0 Hypocalcemia
★ 113.0 Hyperkalemia
114.0 Hypokalemia
115.0 Sodium & Magnesium Imbalances

★ High-Yield Topic

KG.MD Ultimate EKG Breakdown Contents

Part VII: Artifacts
16.0 Einthoven's Triangle
17.0 Left Arm-Right Arm Lead Reversal
18.0 Left Arm-Left Leg Lead Reversal
19.0 Right Arm-Left Leg Lead Reversal
20.0 Left Arm-Right Leg Lead Reversal
21.0 Right Arm-Right Leg Lead Reversal
22.0 Left Leg-Right Leg Lead Reversal
23.0 Bilateral Arm-Leg Lead Reversal
24.0 Precordial (Chest) Lead Reversal
25.0 Identifying the Culprit Electrode of Artifact
26.0 Motion Artifact
27.0 Muscle Artifact

Part VIII: Inherited Arrhythmia Disorders
★128.0 Brugada Syndrome
129.0 Long QT Syndrome
130.0 Short QT Syndrome
131.0 Arrhythmogenic Right Ventricular Dysplasia

Part IX: Miscellaneous
★132.0 Hypothermia
133.0 Intracranial Hemorrhage
★134.0 Early Repolarization
★135.0 Acute Pericarditis
★136.0 Pericardial Effusion & Cardiac Tamponade

★ High-Yield Topic

EKG.MD Ultimate EKG Breakdown Content

Part X: Congenital Heart Disease

137.0 Congenital Heart Disease
138.0 Atrial Septal Defects
139.0 Ostium Secundum Atrial Septal Defect
140.0 Ostium Primum Atrial Septal Defect
141.0 Sinus Venosus Atrial Septal Defect
142.0 Atrioventricular Septal Defect (AV Canal)
143.0 Ventricular Septal Defect
144.0 Patent Ductus Arteriosus
145.0 Aortopulmonary Window
146.0 Pulmonary Valve Stenosis
147.0 Aortic Valve Stenosis
148.0 L-Transposition of the Great Vessels
149.0 Anomalous Left Coronary Artery from the Pulmonary Artery
150.0 Anomalous Origin of Left or Right Coronary Artery from the Contralateral Sinus of Valsalva
151.0 Left Ventricular Noncompaction
152.0 D-Transposition of the Great Arteries
153.0 Tetralogy of Fallot
154.0 Truncus Arteriosus
155.0 Pulmonary Atresia with Intact Ventricular Se
156.0 Ebstein's Anomaly
157.0 Tricuspid Atresia
158.0 Hypoplastic Left Heart Syndrome
159.0 Single Ventricle Defects
160.0 Fontan Palliation

Welcome to the Ultimate EKG Breakdown

Part I: The Basics

TOPICS:

★ 1.0 Cardiac Anatomy & Circulation
★ 2.0 Electrical Conduction System of the Heart
   3.0 Action Potential & Automaticity
★ 4.0 Vectors & Electrical Axis
★ 5.0 Electrodes
★ 6.0 Standard Leads
   7.0 Right-sided Leads
   8.0 Posterior Leads
★ 9.0 ECG Paper
★ 10.0 Standard 12-Lead ECG
★ 11.0 Localizing ECG Leads
★ 12.0 Basic Terms
★ 13.0 Cardiac Cycle & Complex Formation
   14.0 P Wave
   15.0 Ta Wave

16.0 PR Segment
17.0 PR Interval
18.0 QRS Complex
19.0 QRS Nomenclature
20.0 Intrinsicoid Deflection
21.0 ST Segment
22.0 T Wave
23.0 QT Interval
24.0 U Wave
25.0 TP Segment
★ 26.0 PP & RR Intervals
★ 27.0 Determining Regularity
★ 28.0 Determining Rate
★ 29.0 Determining Axis (Frontal Plane)
★ 30.0 Transitional Zone
★ 31.0 R Wave Progression

★ High-Yield Topic

EKG.

Cardiac Anatomy & Circulation

Key Points
- rt = 4-chamber pump (2 atria + 2 ventricles)
  - Made up of 2-3 billion cardiomyocytes
  - Location: center of chest cavity
  - Directed inferiorly, leftward, & anteriorly
  - RV = most anterior portion

- culation: 1 closed system
  - Veins: bring blood *to* heart
  - Arteries: take blood *away from* heart
  - Atria empty into corresponding ventricles
  - RA → RV → PA → lungs → PV → LA →
  - LV → Ao → body → IVC/SVC → RA...

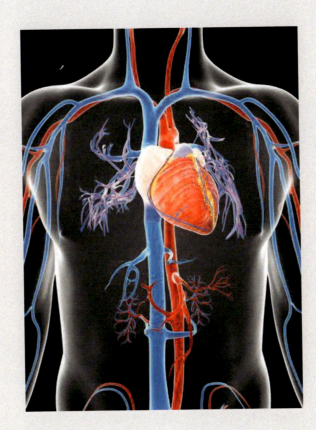
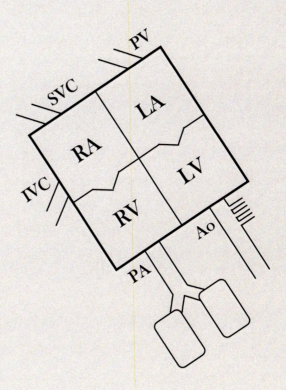

1.0

Electrical Conduction System of the Heart

Key Points

- Electrical conduction system:
  - Creates & transmits organized electrical impulse
  - SA node → internodal pathways (+ Bachmann bundle) → AVN → His bundle → RBB + LBB (LAF, LPF) → Purkinje fibers → cardiomyocytes

- PM cell:
  - Dictates rate
  - Fastest PM controls heart
  - Back-up system ("safety net")

- General intrinsic rates (adults):
  - Sinus node/atria: 60-100 BPM
  - AV junction: 40-60 BPM
  - Ventricles: 20-40 BPM

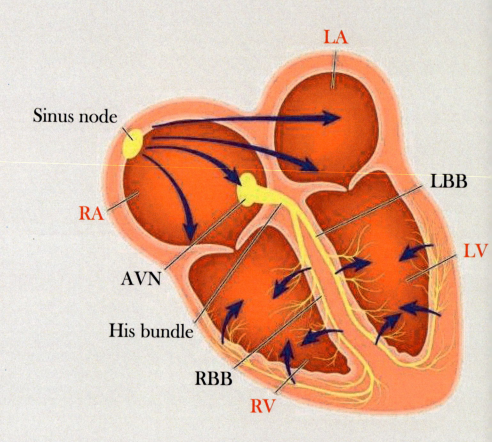

Action Potential & Automaticity

Key Points

AP = depolarization (activation) + repolarization (recovery)
- Occurs in all cardiomyocytes, but varies in cell type
- Flow of electrically charged ions → electrical current + electrical conductors (ie, surrounding fluids & tissues) → electrodes → ECG
- Note: EP of conducting system too small to be detected; thus, atrial/ventricular activity recorded

SA node:
- Pacemaker potential (4) = Na^+ influx at resting state
- ...Na^+ influx (4) → AP near -40 mV + Ca^{2+} influx + depolarization (0) → K^+ efflux → repolarization (3)...
- AP propagates via gap junctions

Contractile myocyte:
- True resting potential (4) & thus must be stimulated
- ...K^+ efflux (resting state, -90 mV) → cell stimulated → rapid Na^+ influx → depolarization (0) → K^+ efflux → early repolarization (1) → Ca^{2+} influx → plateau phase (2) → Ca^{2+} channels close + K^+ efflux → repolarization (3)...
- Total AP duration: atria ~200 ms; ventricles ~300 ms
- Absolute RP: no stimulus can trigger new AP
- Relative RP: strong stimulus can trigger new AP

Sinoatrial node AP

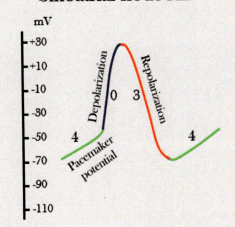

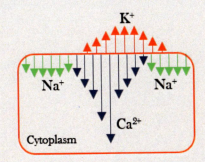

Contractile myocyte AP

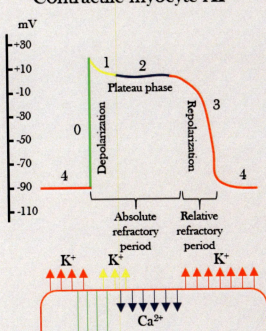

Vectors & Electrical Axis

Key Points

- Vector:
  - Electrical impulse created by cardiomyocyte
  - Energy + direction of impulse

- Resultant vector:
  - Same direction: add
  - Opposite direction: subtract
  - At angle: add/subtract + factor in direction

- Electrical axis:
  - Represented by resultant vector
  - Wave/segment = vector sum passing electrode

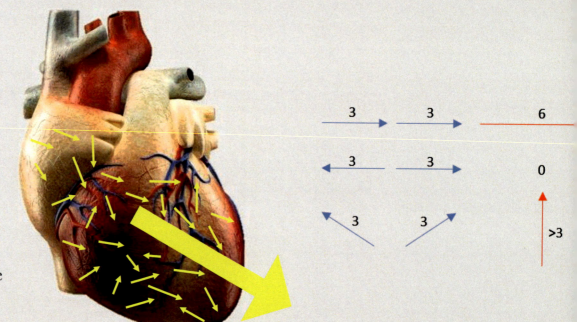

Electrodes

Key Points

Electrodes: sense electrical activity
- ✓ Standard 12-lead ECG: 10 electrodes (4 on limbs + 6 on precordium) monitor 12 leads
- ✓ "Cameras" providing 3-D image of heart's electrical activity → EKG

EKG detection of positive impulse moving:
- ✓ Away → negative deflection
- ✓ Toward → positive deflection
- ✓ Perpendicular → isoelectric deflection

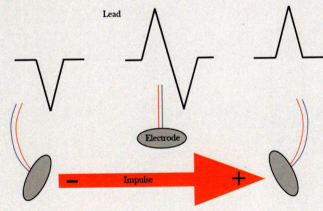

Standard Leads

Key Points

- Lead basics:
  - ✓ Standard ECG: 12 leads
  - ✓ 2 lead systems: hexaxial & precordial
  - ✓ Positive end gets lead name

- (1) Hexaxial system: frontal plane
  - ✓ 6 limb/extremity leads
  - ✓ Leads: I, II, III, aVR, aVL, aVR
  - ✓ Each lead 30° apart

- (2) Precordial system: horizontal plane
  - ✓ 6 precordial/chest leads
  - ✓ Leads: (R) V1, V2, V3, V4, V5, V6 (L)
  - ✓ Each lead 20° apart

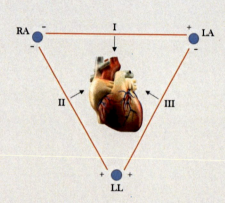
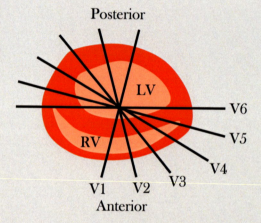
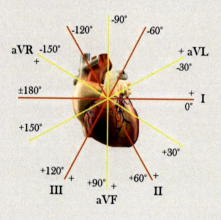
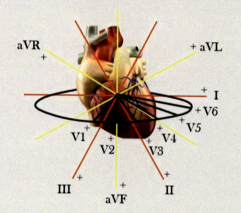
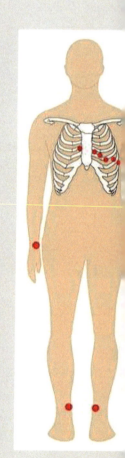

Right-Sided Leads

Key Points
Right-sided leads: **V3R-V6R**
- ✓ Provide right-lateral view of heart
- ✓ Mirror image of V3-V6
- ✓ Consider in setting of inferior MI
- ✓ Useful for diagnosing **RV MI**

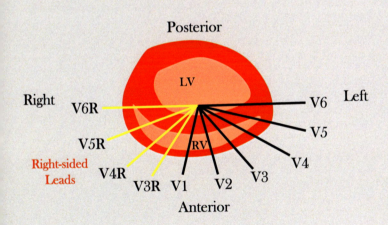

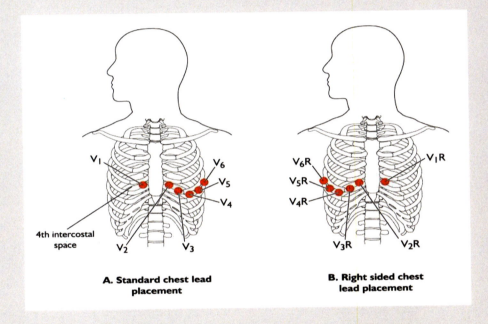

A. Standard chest lead placement

B. Right sided chest lead placement

Posterior Leads

Key Points
- Posterior leads: V7-V10
  - Provide posterior view of heart
  - Continuation of V1-V6
  - Consider in setting of STD in V1-V3 w/o RBBB
  - Useful for diagnosing posterior MI

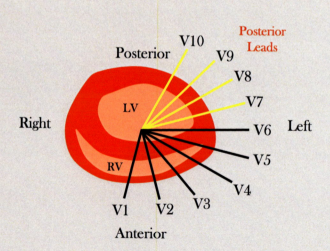
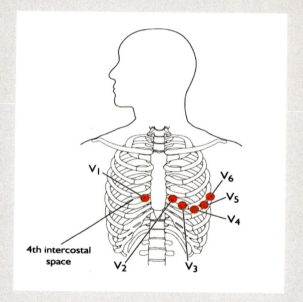
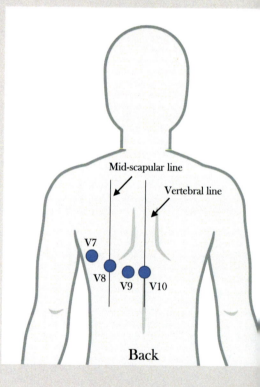

ECG Paper

Key Points

ECG paper: grid system
- 1 big box/square = 25 small boxes/squares
- 1 small box = 1 mm → 1 big box = 5 mm x 5 mm

Horizontal = time (s, ms)
- 1 mm (1 small box) = 0.04 s, 40 ms
- 5 mm (1 big box) = 0.2 s, 200 ms
- 5 big boxes = (0.2 s) x 5 = 1 s

Vertical = voltage (mm, mV)
- 1 mm (1 small box) = 0.1 mV
- 10 mm (2 big boxes) = 1 mV

Calibration:
- Standard: 10 mm (1 mV) x 5 mm (0.2 s); 25 mm/s
- Half-standard: "stair-like" structure; ↓ voltage

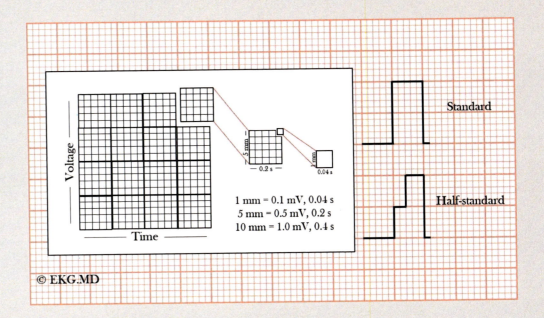

Standard 12-Lead ECG

Key Points
- Standard 12-lead ECG:
  - ✓ 6 limb leads: I, II, III, aVR, aVL, aVF
  - ✓ 6 precordial leads: V1-V6
  - ✓ ± Rhythm strip(s)
  - ✓ Total duration: 10 s; each lead = 2.5 s
  - ✓ Temporal relationship

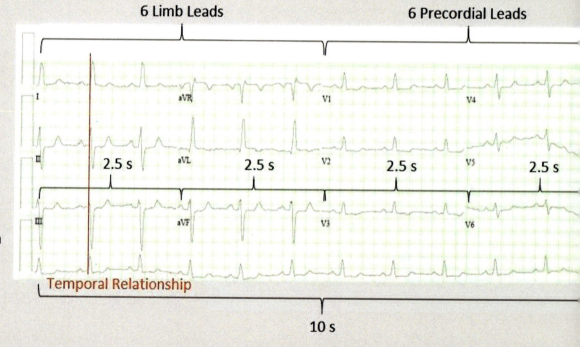

Localizing ECG Leads

Leads	Heart Region
I, III, aVF	Inferior
V1-V2	Septal
V3-V4	Anterior
aVL, V5-V6	Left lateral
V3R-V6R	Right lateral
V7-V10	Posterior

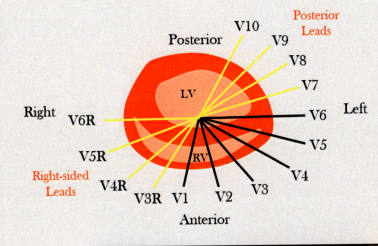
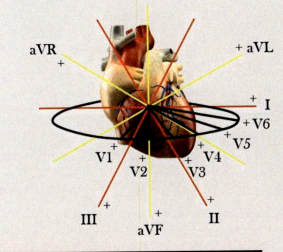

I Lateral	aVR	V1 Septal	V4 Anterior
II Inferior	aVL Lateral	V2 Septal	V5 Lateral
III Inferior	aVF Inferior	V3 Anterior	V6 Lateral

11.0

Basic Terms

Key Points

- Wave: +/- deflection from baseline (specific electrical event)
  - Pw = 1st defection of complex; atrial depolarization
  - Qw = 1st negative deflection after P wave
  - Rw = 1st positive deflection after P wave
  - Sw = 1st negative deflection after R wave
  - Tw = deflection after QRS; ventricular repolarization
  - Uw = deflection after T wave (not often present)

- Interval: time b/t 2 ECG events (eg, PR, QRS, QT, RR, PP)
  - PR interval = Pw + PR segment
  - QT interval = QRS + ST segment + Tw

- Segment: time b/t 2 specific points on ECG (eg, PR, ST, TP)

- QRS complex: Qw + Rw + Sw; ventricular depolarization

- Junction (J) point: QRS ends & ST segment begins

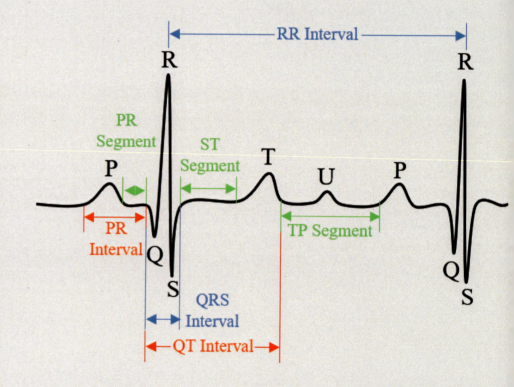

Cardiac Cycle & Complex Formation

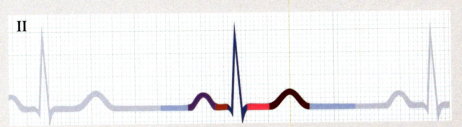

Key Points

Baseline: sinus nodal cells slowly depolarize until threshold reached & then initiate impulse, spreading through internodal pathways to AVN

PR interval: Pw + PR segment
- ✓ Cardiac events: atria depolarize (RA before LA) + AVN physiologic block + atria repolarize

QRS complex: ventricular depolarization
- ✓ Septal Qw: upper ventricular septal depolarizes from L-to-R
- ✓ Rw: main LV depolarizes
- ✓ Sw: remaining LV depolarizes

ST segment: time b/t ventricular depolarization & repolarization

Tw: ventricular repolarization
- ✓ Early Tw: *absolute* refractory period (depolarized > repolarized ventricular cells → refractory to new impulse)
- ✓ Late Tw: *relative* refractory period (repolarized > depolarized ventricular cells → ready to receive new impulse)

TP segment: heart relaxes, automaticity continues, & cycle repeats

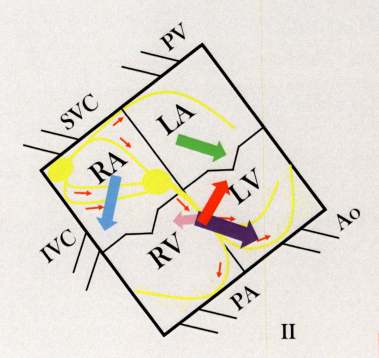

13.0

P Wave

Key Points

- Pw: 1st +/- deflection & start of cardiac cycle
  - ✓ Cardiac event: atrial depolarization
  - ✓ Begins when sinus node (normal) or neighboring atrial PMs fire
  - ✓ Includes impulse transmission through internodal pathway, Bachmann bundle, & atrial myocytes
  - ✓ Impulse transmission: RA → interatrial septum → LA
- Pw morphology: smooth contour; monophasic in II; biphasic in V1
- Pw axis (frontal plane): 0° to +75° (leftward & inferiorly)
  - ✓ Initial Pw: upper RA depol. (directed anteriorly)
  - ✓ Terminal Pw: LA + inferior RA wall depol. (directed posteriorly)
  - ✓ Upright in I, II, aVF, V4-V6; inverted in aVR; variable in others
- Pw duration: 0.08-0.11 s (80-110 ms)
- Pw amplitude:
  - ✓ Limb leads: <2.5 mm
  - ✓ Precordial leads: + component <1.5 mm, – component <1.0 mm
- Pw abnormalities: best seen in II, III, aVF, & V1 b/c most prominent

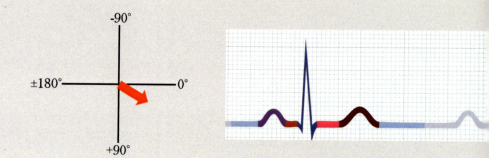

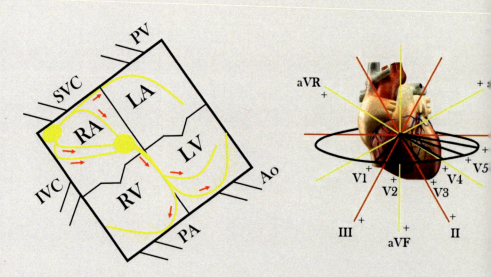

Ta Wave

Key Points

Ta wave: "atrial Tw"
- ✓ Cardiac event: atrial repolarization (occurs in same direction as atrial depolarization)
- ✓ Wave orientation: opposite to Pw (atrial depolarization)
- ✓ Often not visible (electrically insignificant or buried w/in QRS)
- ✓ May be present (1) if no QRS after Pw (eg, AV dissociation) or (2) as PRD/STD (eg, pericarditis, atrial MI, sinus tachycardia)
- ✓ Can affect baseline if present (ie, PR segment)

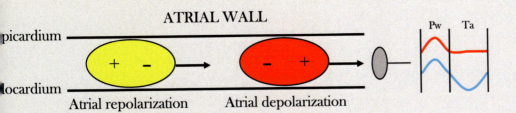

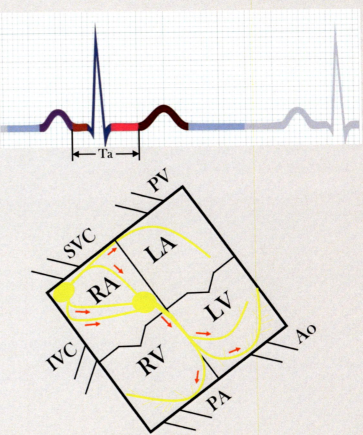

PR Segment

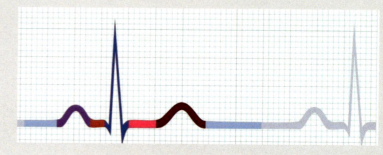

Key Points

- PR segment: represents time from end of Pw to start of QRS
  - ✓ Cardiac event: impulse transmission through AVN, His bundle, bundle branches, & ventricular Purkinje system ± atrial repolarization
  - ✓ Considered baseline for determining STE/STD

- AVN conduction delay makes up most of PR segment
  - ✓ W/o delay: atria & ventricles would contract simultaneously → ineffective blood flow from atria to ventricles

- PR segment: often flat, isoelectric, & located along baseline
  - ✓ PR depression: normal <0.8 mm
  - ✓ PR elevation: normal <0.5 mm
  - ✓ PRE/PRD DDx: normal variant, pericarditis, atrial MI, atrial repolarization (Ta wave)

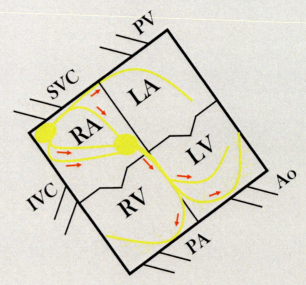

PR Interval

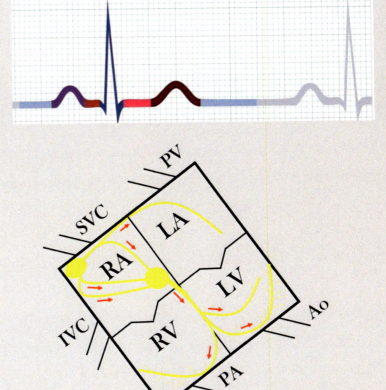

Key Points

PR interval: represents time from Pw onset to QRS onset
- PR interval = Pw + PR segment ± Ta
- "PQ interval" used interchangeably if Qw initial wave of QRS
- Cardiac event: [impulse initiation] + [atrial depolarization & repolarization] + [transmission through AVN, His bundle, bundle branches, & ventricular Purkinje system]
- Most of it reflects slow AVN conduction (proximal to His bundle)

PR interval duration: 0.12-0.2 s (120-200 ms)
- Measure in leads with largest, widest Pw & longest QRS interval
- Tends to ↑ w/ age
- Short PR interval (<120 ms): consider normal variant, ventricular preexcitation (accessory pathway), or junctional/low atrial rhythm
- Prolonged PR interval (>200 ms): consider normal variant or AVB

QRS Complex

Key Points

- QRS complex:
  - ✓ Cardiac event: ventricular depolarization
  - ✓ Ventricular activation sequence:
    1. Septal & paraseptal (rightward & anteriorly)
    2. Ventricular free wall (leftward)
    3. Posterobasal septum & posterior ventricles (superiorly + anteriorly/posteriorly)
- QRS interval (duration): 0.07-0.11 s (70-110 ms)
  - ✓ Measure in lead w/ widest QRS (precordial leads – V2, V3)
  - ✓ Males > females
  - ✓ Large & tall > small & short individuals
- QRS axis (frontal plane): -30° to +105° (leftward & inferiorly)
  - ✓ Shifts leftward w/ ↑ age
- QRS amplitude (height):
  - ✓ Maximum: 20-30 mm in II, 25-30 mm in precordial leads
  - ✓ Minimum: <5 mm in limb leads, <10 mm in precordial leads
  - ✓ Males > females
  - ✓ African Americans > Caucasians
  - ✓ Younger & thinner > older & obese individuals
  - ✓ Precordial > limb leads

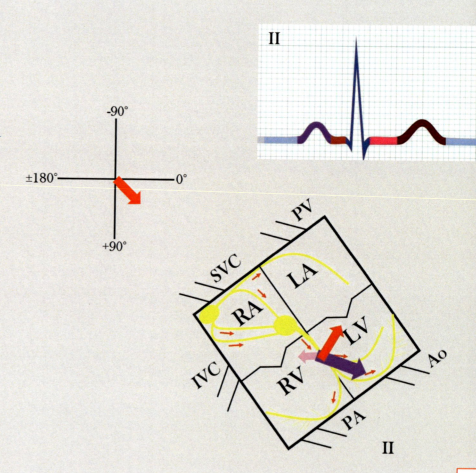

QRS Nomenclature

Key Points

QRS nomenclature:
- ✓ Qw: 1st negative deflection after Pw (not always present)
- ✓ Rw: 1st positive deflection after Pw
- ✓ Sw: 1st negative deflection below baseline after Rw
- ✓ Small letters (q, r, s): small amplitude deflections
- ✓ >1 of same wave = "prime" (') wave (prime, double prime, etc.)
- ✓ No Rw = QS complex

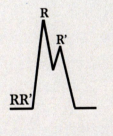
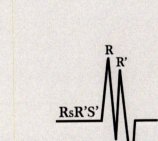
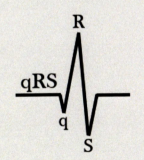
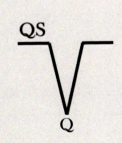
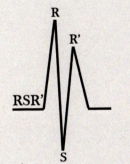

19.0

Intrinsicoid Deflection

Key Points

- Intrinsicoid deflection: time from **QRS** onset to Rw peak
  - Cardiac event: impulse transmission from Purkinje network in endocardium to epicardium surface directly under electrode

- Intrinsicoid deflection duration:
  - R-precordial leads (V1-V2): <0.035 s (35 ms)
  - L-precordial leads (V5-V6): <0.045 s (45 ms)
  - Note: shorter in R-precordial leads due to thinner RV (vs. LV)

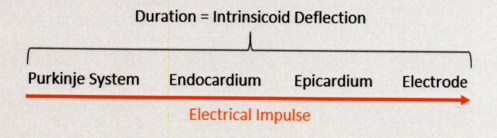

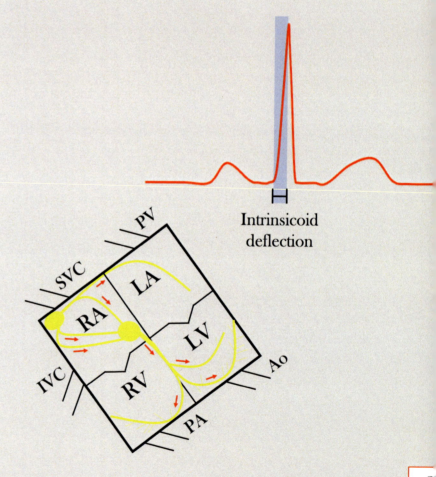

ST Segment

Key Points

ST segment: from QRS end (J point, ST junction) to Tw onset
- ✓ Cardiac event: electrically neutral period b/t ventricular depolarization (QRS) & ventricular repolarization (Tw); ventricular contraction maintained to expel blood

ST segment located at baseline, but possible normal variation
- ✓ Limb leads: <1 mm STE or STD
- ✓ Precordial leads:
  - ✓ STE: V2-V3 (most prominent) ≤3 mm, V5-V6: <1 mm
  - ✓ STD: always abnormal
- ✓ Posterior leads: 0.5-1.0 mm STE at 80 ms after J point

ST-segment morphology
- ✓ Certain morphologies more common in specific conditions
- ✓ Different STD & STE morphologies possible

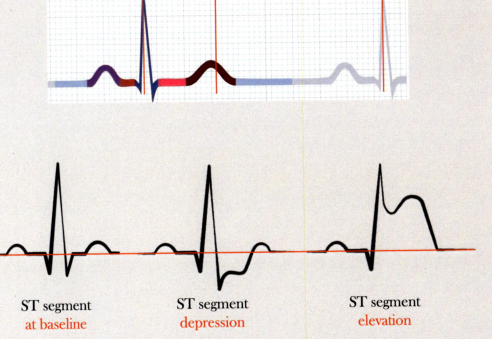

ST segment at baseline | ST segment depression | ST segment elevation

T Wave

Key Points

➤ Tw: next +/- deflection after ST segment
  - ✓ Cardiac event: ventricular repolarization
  - ✓ Early Tw: *absolute* refractory period (depolarized > repolarized ventricular cells → refractory to new impulse)
  - ✓ Late Tw: *relative* refractory period (repolarized > depolarized ventricular cells → ready to receive new impulse)
  - ✓ End Tw: "supranormal" (hyperexcitable) period" (weak stimulus can cause action potential)

➤ Tw orientation: same as QRS (b/c repolarization wave travels opposite to depolarization wave – ie, epicardium to endocardium)

➤ Tw morphology: asymmetric w/ SLOW upstroke/downstroke & more RAPID downstroke/upstroke

➤ Tw axis (frontal plane): -30° to +105° (leftward & inferiorly ± anteriorly)
  - ✓ Upright in I, II, V3-V6; inverted in aVR ± V1; variable in others

➤ Tw amplitude:
  - ✓ Limb leads: ≤6 mm
  - ✓ Precordial leads: ≤12 mm
  - ✓ ≤2/3, but >10% Rw
  - ✓ Males > females; ↓ w/ ↑ age

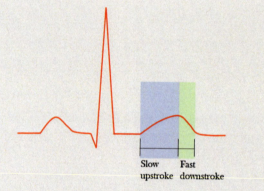
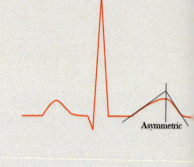
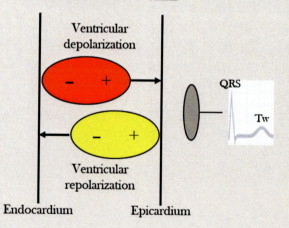
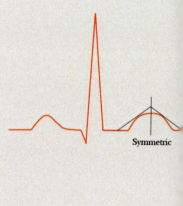

QT Interval

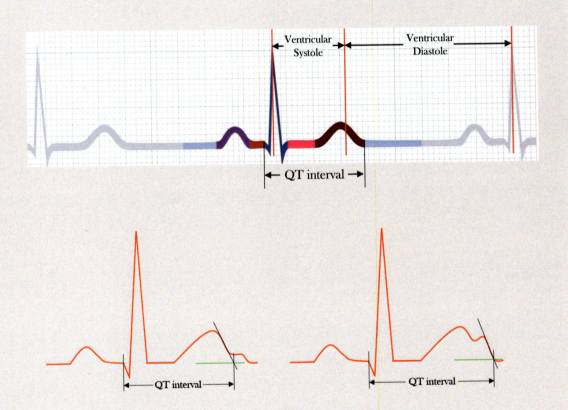

Key Points

QT interval: represents time from QRS onset to end of Tw
- ✓ QT interval = QRS + ST segment + Tw
- ✓ Cardiac event: ventricular depolarization + ventricular repolarization (note: all of ventricular systole)

QT interval duration: variable (age, sex, HR, electrolytes)
- ✓ In general: normal QT <½ preceding RR interval
- ✓ Best measured in II, V5, or V6 (use maximum interval)
- ✓ If TU fusion: use maximum slope-intercept method to define end of Tw (include Uw >1 mm)
- ✓ Females > males
- ✓ Inversely related to HR (↓ QT w/ ↑ HR; ↑ QT w/ ↓ HR)

QTc interval: attempts to correct for QT variation w/ HR
- ✓ Improves detection of patients at ↑ risk of arrhythmias
- ✓ Bazett's formula: $QTc = \frac{QT}{\sqrt{RR}}$
- ✓ Normal (varies): males <440 ms; females <460 ms; >350 ms
- ✓ QTc >500 ms: ↑ risk of torsades de pointes

U Wave

Key Points

- Uw: small, low-frequency diastolic deflection
  - If present, often begins w/ 2nd heart sound at onset of ventricular relaxation & after end of Tw but before next Pw
  - Cardiac event: unclear
  - Uw ascent duration ≤ descent duration

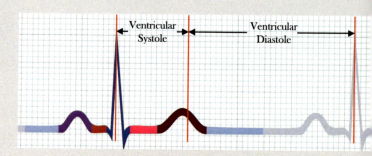

- Uw orientation: same direction as Tw

- Uw axis: similar to Tw (leftward, inferiorly ± anteriorly)

- Uw amplitude: less than Tw & rarely >0.2 mV (2 mm)
  - Varies directly w/ Tw amplitude
  - Often greatest in V2-V3

- Clinical significance:
  - Often benign; seen in bradycardia
  - Potential sign of hypokalemia (rules out hyperkalemia)
  - May cause inaccurate QT interval measurement (TU fusion)

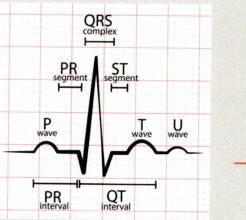
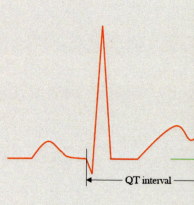

TP Segment

Key Points

TP segment: represents time end of Tw to Pw onset
- Normally isoelectric & located at baseline
- Cardiac event: occurs during ventricular diastole
- Formerly considered reference line for ST deviation (now PR segment; may be useful if PR segment abnormally deviated)
- ↑ HR → shortens TP segment (may be difficult to visualize)

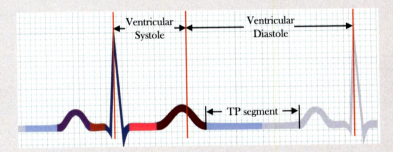

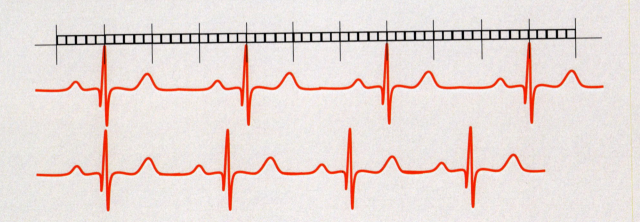

25.0

PP & RR Intervals

Key Points

- PP interval:
  - Represents time b/t identical points on 2 consecutive Pw
  - Assists in evaluating rhythm abnormalities (eg, atrial flutter, 2nd-degree AVB Mobitz I, 3rd-degree AVB)

- RR interval:
  - Represents time b/t Rw of 2 consecutive QRS complexes
  - Assists in evaluating rhythm regularity (regular vs. irregular)

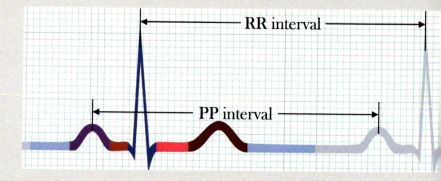

Determining Regularity

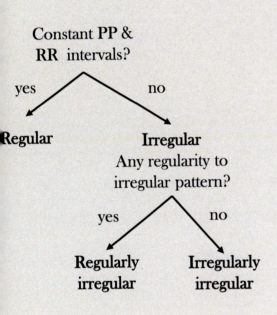
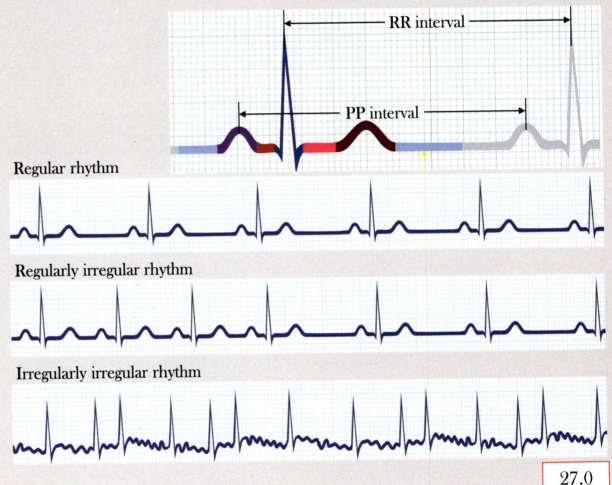

Determining Rate

Key Points

- Rate: frequency of P waves (atrial) or QRS complexes (ventricular)
- Determining rate: regular/irregular + fast/slow rhythms
  - Standard 12-lead ECG = 10 s
  - HR = (# of Pw or QRS complexes in rhythm strip) x 6
- Regular rhythms: "300-150-100-75-60-50"
  - HR = 300 / (# thick lines b/t PP or RR interval)
- Regular, fast rhythms:
  - HR = 1500 / (# small boxes b/t PP or RR interval)

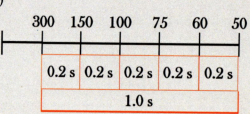
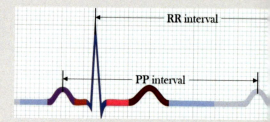
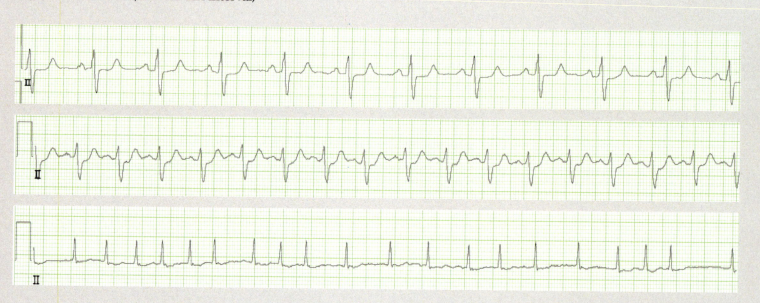

Determining Axis (Frontal Plane)

Key Points

Electrical axis: represents general flow of electrical impulses through heart from sinus node to Purkinje fibers (ie, direction of resultant vector)
- ✓ X-Y axis (frontal plane): use limb leads (I, II, aVF)
- ✓ Z-axis: use precordial leads

Ventricular (QRS) axis:
- ✓ Normal axis: -30° to +105°
- ✓ LAD: -30° to -90°
- ✓ RAD: +105° to +180°
- ✓ Extreme axis deviation: -90° to -180°
- ✓ Indeterminate: cannot define axis (I, II, aVF isoelectric)

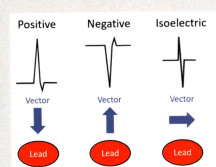
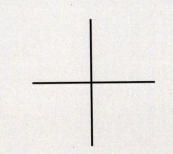
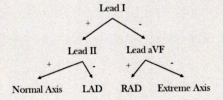
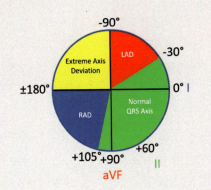
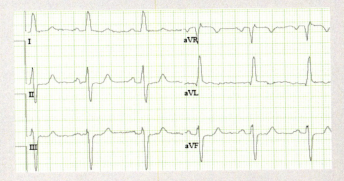
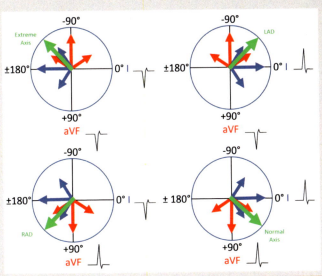

29.0

Transitional Zone

Key Points

- Transitional zone: precordial lead where **QRS** transitions from mostly negative to mostly positive (actual transition: **QRS** isoelectric)
  - ✓ Transition b/t V3-V4 = normal transition
  - ✓ Transition before V3 = CCW rotation (early transition; rightward shift)
  - ✓ Transition after V4 = CW rotation (late transition; leftward shift)
- Clinical significance: misplaced leads; anatomical variations (eg, vertical heart)
  - ✓ CW rotation more often significant (eg, anterior MI, COPD, dilated CM) than CCW rotation (eg, posterior MI, RVH)

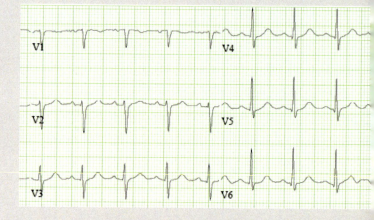

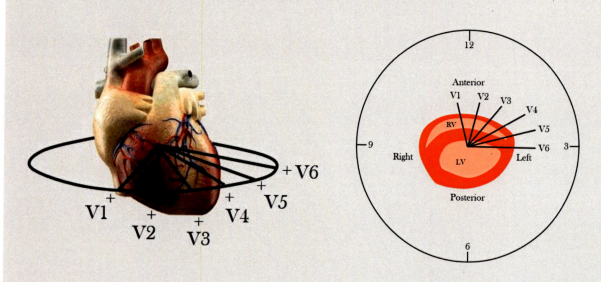

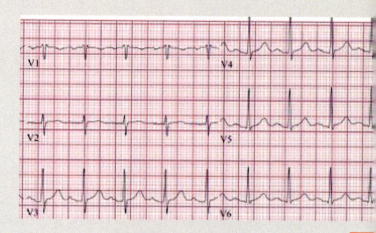

R Wave Progression

Key Points

Rw progression:
- ➢ Normal: ↑ Rw amplitude from V1-V5
- ✓ Absent/poor: Sw > Rw amplitude from V1-V5 (eg, anterior MI)
- ✓ Reverse: ↓ Rw amplitude from V1-V5 (eg, RVH)

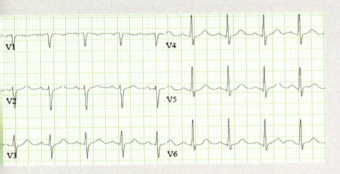
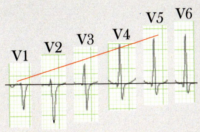
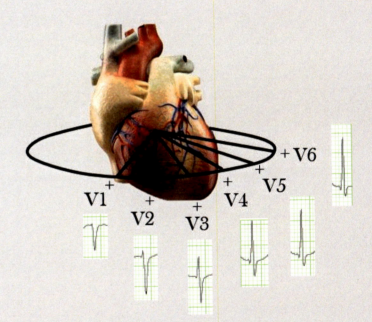
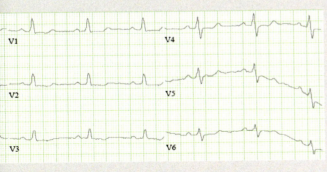
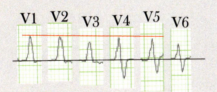

Part II: Rhythms

TOPICS:
32.0 Approach to Rhythms

Sinus Rhythms
★ 33.0 Normal Sinus Rhythm
★ 34.0 Sinus Arrhythmia
★ 35.0 Sinus Bradycardia
★ 36.0 Sinus Tachycardia
37.0 Sinus Pause & Arrest
38.0 Sinoatrial Exit Block

Atrial Rhythms
★ 39.0 Premature Atrial Contraction
40.0 Ectopic Atrial Tachycardia
★ 41.0 Wandering Atrial Pacemaker
★ 42.0 Multifocal Atrial Tachycardia
★ 43.0 Atrial Flutter
★ 44.0 Atrial Fibrillation

AV Junctional & Nodal Rhythms
★ 45.0 Premature Junctional Contraction
★ 46.0 Junctional Escape Beat
★ 47.0 Junctional Escape Rhythm
48.0 Accelerated Junctional Rhythm
49.0 AV Nodal Reentrant Tachycardia
★ 50.0 Wolff-Parkinson-White (WPW) Syndrome
51.0 Lown-Ganong-Levine (LGL) Syndrome
52.0 AV Reentrant Tachycardia

Ventricular Rhythms
★ 53.0 Premature Ventricular Contraction
★ 54.0 Ventricular Escape Beat
★ 55.0 Ventricular Escape (Idioventricular) R
★ 56.0 Accelerated Idioventricular Rhythm
57.0 Fusion & Capture Beats
58.0 Brugada's & Josephson's Signs
★ 59.0 Ventricular Tachycardia
60.0 Reentrant Ventricular Tachycardia
★ 61.0 Torsades de Pointes
★ 62.0 Ventricular Flutter
★ 63.0 Ventricular Fibrillation
★ 64.0 Asystole
★ 65.0 Pulseless Electrical Activity
★ 66.0 Pacemaker Rhythms

★ High-Yield Topic

EKG.

Approach to Rhythms

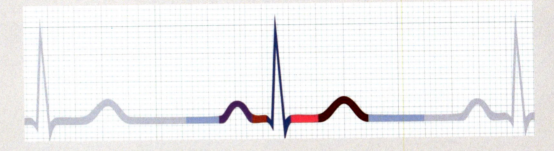

Rhythm	Overview, mechanism, causes, clinical significance, etc.
gularity	Regular vs. irregular
e	Expected rate (BPM)
	Morphology, axis, configuration
QRS ratio	1:1, 2:1, etc.
interval	Shortened, normal, prolonged ± constant
S interval	Normal or prolonged
ouping	Present or not
opped beats	Present or not

Rhythms
- ✓ Sinus rhythms
- ✓ Atrial arrhythmias
- ✓ AV junctional arrhythmias
- ✓ AV reentrant arrhythmias
- ✓ Ventricular arrhythmias
- ✓ AV blocks

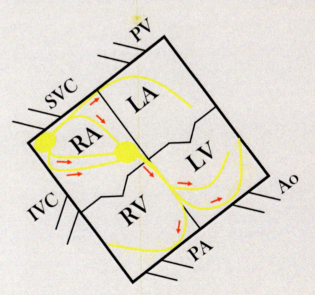

Normal Sinus Rhythm

Normal Sinus Rhythm	• Default heart rhythm • Originates from sinoatrial (SA, sinus) node at normal rate • Intervals constant & w/in normal limits • May occur w/ ventricular escape rhythm or AV dissociation
Regularity	Regular
Rate	60-100 BPM (adults; age-dependent in children) • Newborn: 90-155 BPM; 1-12 mos: 100-170 BPM; 1-3 y/o: 90-150 BPM; 3-5 y/o: 70-140 BPM; 5-12 y/o: 60-130 BPM; 12-16 y/o: 60-120 BPM; 16+ y/o: 60-100 BPM
Pw	• Present w/ constant morphology • Axis (frontal plane): 0° to +75° (leftward & inferior) • Configuration: upright in I, II, V4-V6; inverted in aVR; upright, inverted, or biphasic (positive-negative) in V1-V2; variable in III & aVL (related to respiratory cycles)
Pw:QRS ratio	1:1
PR interval	Constant, normal (120-200 ms)
QRS interval	Normal (70-110 ms)
Grouping	None
Dropped beats	None

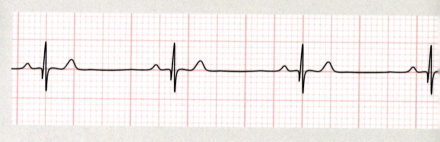

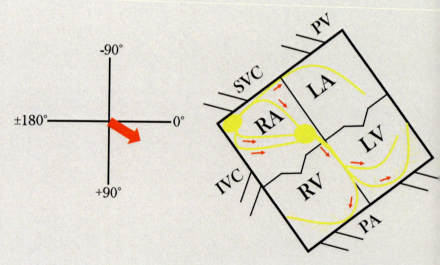

Sinus Arrhythmia

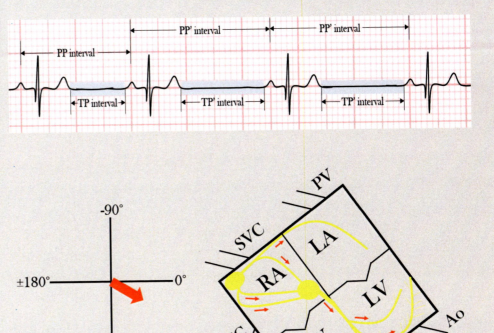

Sinus arrhythmia	• Variation in sinus rate → irregular ventricular rate • Originates from sinoatrial (SA, sinus) node • PP interval variation >160 ms • PP, RR, & TP intervals vary
Regularity	Regularly irregular (varies w/ respiration; ↑ vagal tone → ↓ HR) • Inspiration: ↓ vagal tone → ↑ HR • Expiration: ↑ vagal tone (returns to normal) → ↓ HR
Rate	60-100 BPM
P wave	• Sinus Pw present w/ constant morphology • Axis (frontal plane): 0° to +75° (leftward & inferior) • Configuration: upright in I, II, V4-V6; inverted in aVR; upright, inverted, or biphasic (positive-negative) in V1-V2; variable in III & aVL (related to respiratory cycles)
P:QRS ratio	1:1
PR interval	Constant, normal (120-200 ms)
QRS interval	Normal (70-110 ms)
Grouping	None
Dropped beats	None

34.0

Sinus Bradycardia

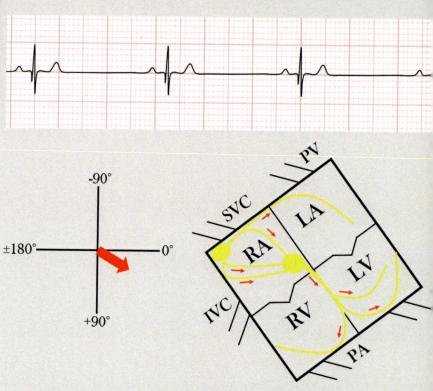

Sinus Bradycardia	• Originates from sinoatrial (SA, sinus) node at slow rate • PR, QRS, QT intervals normal ± slightly prolonged (WNL) • Causes: sleep; ↑ vagal tone (athletes); inferior MI; ↓ T; ↑ K; ↑ Mg; hypothyroidism; myocarditis; anorexia nervosa; intracranial events; surgical trauma; channelopathy; sinus node dysfunction; meds (eg, βBs, CCBs, digoxin, amiodarone, opiates, barbiturates)
Regularity	Regular
Rate	<60 BPM (adults; age-dependent in children) • Newborn: 90-155 BPM; 1-12 mos: 100-170 BPM; 1-3 y/o: 90-150 BPM; 3-5 y/o: 70-140 BPM; 5-12 y/o: 60-130 BPM; 12-16 y/o: 60-120 BPM; 16+ y/o: 60-100 BPM
Pw	• Sinus Pw present w/ constant morphology • Axis (frontal plane): 0° to +75° (leftward & inferior) • Configuration: upright in I, II, V4-V6; inverted in aVR; upright, inverted, or biphasic (positive-negative) in V1-V2; variable in III & aVL (related to respiratory cycles)
Pw:QRS ratio	1:1
PR interval	Constant, normal (120-200 ms)
QRS interval	Normal (70-110 ms)
Grouping	None
Dropped beats	None

Sinus Tachycardia

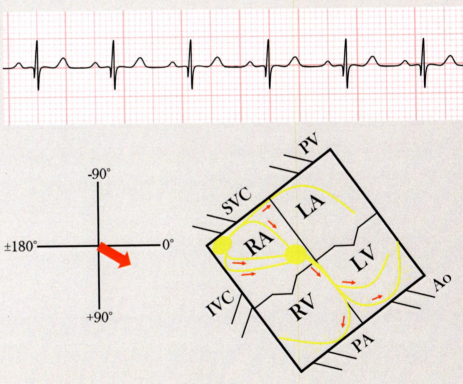

Sinus Tachycardia	• Originates from sinoatrial (SA, sinus) node at fast rate • Causes: exercise; pain; anxiety; hyperthyroidism; ↓O_2; ↑CO_2; ↑H; ↑T; sepsis; ↓vol; pulmonary embolism; meds (eg, β-agonist; sympathomimetics; antimuscarinics; caffeine)
arity	Regular
	>100 BPM (adults; age-dependent in children) • Newborn: 90-155 BPM; 1-12 mos: 100-170 BPM; 1-3 y/o: 90-150 BPM; 3-5 y/o: 70-140 BPM; 5-12 y/o: 60-130 BPM; 12-16 y/o: 60-120 BPM; 16+ y/o: 60-100 BPM
	• Sinus Pw present w/ constant morphology • ↑↑ HR: Pw may be hidden in preceding Tw ('camel hump') • Axis (frontal plane): 0° to +75° (leftward & inferior) • Configuration: upright in I, II, V4-V6; inverted in aVR; upright, inverted, or biphasic (positive-negative) in V1-V2; variable in III & aVL (related to respiratory cycles)
RS ratio	1:1
terval	Constant, normal (120-200 ms)
interval	Normal (70-110 ms)
ping	None
ped beats	None

36.0

Sinus Pause & Arrest

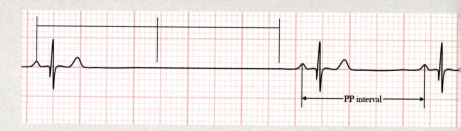

Sinus Pause & Arrest	• Sinus pacemaking (P) cells fail to produce impulse • Sinus pause ← 2-3 s cutoff → sinus arrest • Time interval: not a multiple of normal PP interval • Causes: sick sinus syndrome; ↑ vagal tone (eg, athletes, pain, surgery); inferior MI; myocarditis; meds (eg, βBs, CCBs, digoxin, amiodarone)
Regularity	Irregular
Rate	Varies
Pw	Present except in areas of sinus pause/arrest
Pw:QRS ratio	1:1
PR interval	Constant, normal (120-200 ms)
QRS interval	Normal (70-110 ms)
Grouping	None
Dropped beats	Yes

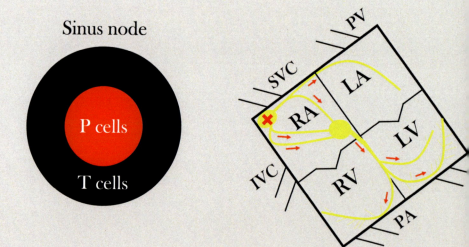

Sinoatrial Exit Block

- SA node depolarizes normally, but transitional (T) cells fail to transmit impulse → intermittent atrial depolarization failure (dropped Pw)
- Various patterns (similar to AV block types)
- Multiple of normal PP intervals (2nd-degree type II)
- Causes: sick sinus syndrome; ↑ vagal tone (eg, athletes, pain, surgery); inferior MI; myocarditis; meds (eg, βBs, CCBs, digoxin, amiodarone)

Sinoatrial Exit Block	
Regularity	Irregular
Rate	Varies
Pw	Present except in areas of dropped beats
Pw:QRS ratio	1:1
PR interval	Constant, normal (120-200 ms)
QRS interval	Normal (70-110 ms)
Grouping	Depends on type
Dropped beats	Yes

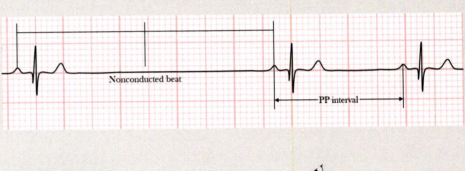

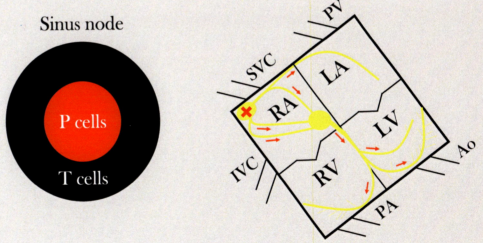

Premature Atrial Contraction

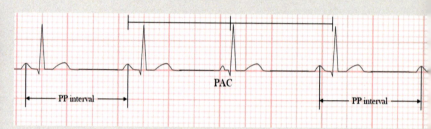

Premature Atrial Contraction	• PM w/in atria fires at faster rate than sinus node • General rule: fastest PM controls heart • "Resets" sinus node → noncompensatory pause (<2x normal PP) • Causes: anxiety; myocardial ischemia; ↓ K; ↓ Mg; meds (eg, sympathomimetics, caffeine, β-agonists, digoxin toxicity) • Clinical significance: common (↓ frequency w/ age); typically benign; ± palpitations; may trigger reentrant tachyarrhythmia
Regularity	Irregular
Rate	Depends on underlying rate
Pw	Present; morphology & axis often different from sinus Pw
Pw:QRS ratio	1:1
PR interval	Varies in PAC, otherwise normal (120-200 ms)
QRS interval	Normal (70-110 ms; similar to underlying rhythm)
Grouping	Sometimes
Dropped beats	None

Nomenclature
- ✓ Unifocal (1 focus & Pw morph) vs. multifocal (>1 foci & Pw morph)
- ✓ Bigeminy (every 2nd); trigeminy (every 3rd); quadrigeminy (every 4th)
- ✓ Couplet (2 consecutive PACs); triplet (3 consecutive PACs)

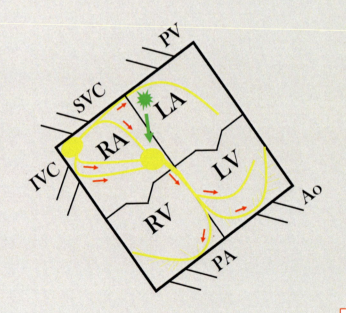

Ectopic Atrial Tachycardia

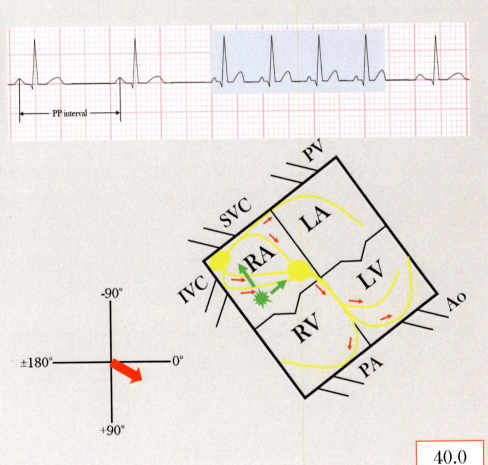

/Automatic Tachycardia	• PM w/in atria fires at faster rate than sinus node (↑ automaticity) • General rule: fastest PM controls heart • Rate variability w/ "warm-up" (initiation) & "cool-down" (termination) distinguishes it from reentrant form • ± transient ST-Tw abnormalities (2/2 rapid rate)
ity	Regular
	>100 BPM (range 100-250 BPM)

	• Present w/ morphology & axis often different from sinus Pw (eg, inverted in II, III, & aVF)
	• ≥3 identical ectopic Pw (identical initiating & tachycardic Pw)
	• Pw in V1 to identify origin:
	   ✓ RA-focus: negative or biphasic (positive-negative)
	   ✓ LA-focus: positive, isoelectric, biphasic (negative-positive)

S ratio	1:1
erval	Often different w/ ectopic focus
nterval	Normal (70-110 ms; unless preexisting IVCD, accessory pathway, or rate-related aberrant conduction)
ing	None
ed beats	None

40.0

Wandering Atrial Pacemaker

Wandering Atrial Pacemaker	• Irregular rhythm arising from ≥3 ectopic foci w/in atria • ↑ vagal tone → slows SA node → faster atrial PMs • Varying PP, PR, & RR intervals • Isoelectric baseline b/t P waves
Regularity	Irregularly irregular
Rate	<100 BPM
Pw	Present w/ ≥3 different Pw morphologies & axes
Pw:QRS ratio	1:1
PR interval	Varies depending on focus
QRS interval	Normal (70-110 ms)
Grouping	None
Dropped beats	None

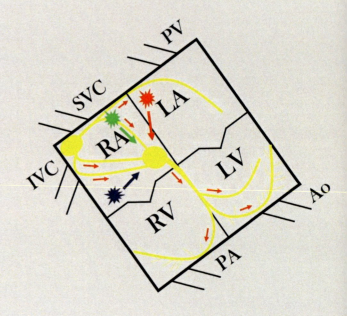

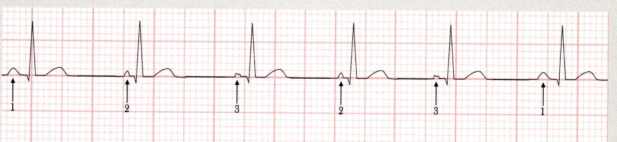

Multifocal Atrial Tachycardia

Multifocal (Chaotic) Atrial Tachycardia	<ul><li>Rapid, irregular rhythm arising from ≥3 ectopic foci w/in atria</li><li>Causes: COPD, CHF (often ill elderly pts w/ respiratory failure)</li><li>Mechanism: ↑ automaticity</li><li>Clinical significance: tends to resolve after treating underlying condition; poor prognostic sign if develops during acute illness</li><li>Varying PP, PR, & RR intervals; isoelectric baseline b/t P waves</li></ul>
Regularity	Irregularly irregular
Rate	≥100 BPM (range 100-250 BPM)
Pw	Present w/ ≥3 different Pw morphologies & axes
Pw:QRS ratio	1:1
PR interval	Varies depending on focus
QRS interval	Normal (70-110 ms); possible aberrant conduction
Grouping	None
Dropped beats	None

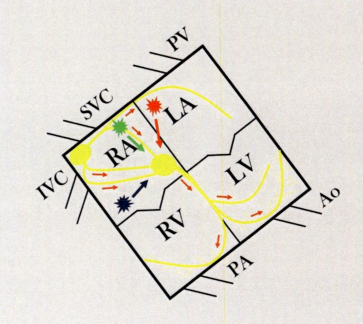

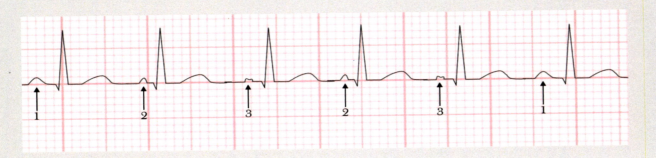

42.0

Atrial Flutter

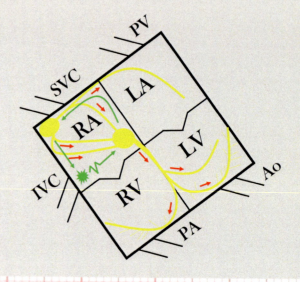

Atrial Flutter	<ul><li>Rapid, regular circulating impulse in RA ± LA; circuit length ∝ RA size</li><li>No isoelectric baseline</li><li>Classified based on (1) anatomical location & (2) direction of reentry circuit<ol><li>Typical (common, type 1): cavotricuspid isthmus<ul><li>CCW reentry: most common; retrograde atrial conduction (inverted Fw in II, III, aVF; positive Fw in V1)</li><li>CW reentry: uncommon; anterograde atrial conduction (positive Fw in II, III, aVF; broad, inverted Fw in V1)</li></ul></li><li>Atypical (uncommon, type 2): 'typical' criteria not met; assoc. w/ ↑ atrial rates & rhythm instability; less responsive to ablation</li></ol></li></ul>
Regularity	Usually regular; may be variable
Rate	<ul><li>Atrial: 250-350 BPM</li><li>Ventricular: 125-175 BPM</li></ul>
Pw	<ul><li>"Saw-tooth" appearing, undulating, & regular Fw (identical throughout)<ul><li>Duration ± amplitude: Fw > Pw</li><li>Look at aVF (± II, III) & V1 (may resemble Pw); turn upside down</li></ul></li></ul>
Pw:QRS ratio	<ul><li>Varies; often 2:1</li><li>"AV block": variable degree, but often regular (eg, 2:1, 3:1, 4:1)<ul><li>If 1:1 conduction: consider accessory pathway → unstable + V-Fib</li><li>Irregular F-F intervals = *atrial flutter w/ variable ventricular response*</li></ul></li></ul>
PR interval	Varies
QRS interval	Normal (70-110 ms; unless preexisting IVCD, accessory pathway, or rate-related aberrant conduction)
Grouping	None
Dropped beats	None

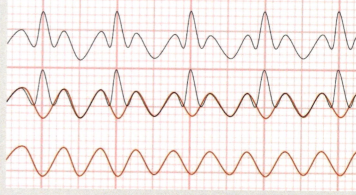

Atrial Fibrillation

- Random, chaotic atrial activity
- Proposed mechanisms: (1) focal activation & (2) multiple wavelets
  - ✓ Initiating event (PAC) + substrate for maintenance (LAE)
- Causes: CHD (esp. if unrepaired); CM; rheumatic HD; toxicity (alcohol, inhalants, illicit drugs); familial form
- Baseline: coarse (≥1 mm in V1), fine (<1 mm in V1), or isoelectric
- Ashman phenomenon: aberrantly conducted beats (RBBB morph in V1) 2/2 long refractory period (based on preceding RR interval)

rity	Irregularly irregular (most common)
	Ventricular rate varies (slow, normal, or fast; if fast = A-Fib w/ RVR)
	No discernable Pw
S ratio	None
erval	None
interval	Normal (70-110 ms; unless preexisting IVCD, accessory pathway, or rate-related aberrant conduction)
ing	None
ed beats	None

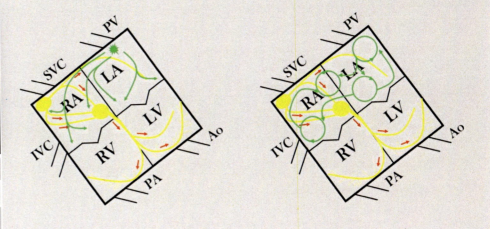

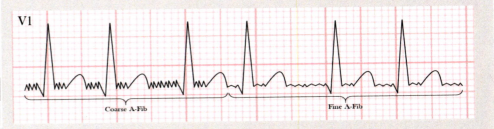

44.0

Premature Junctional Contraction

Premature Junctional Contraction	<ul><li>Early beat originating from ectopic focus w/in AV junction → anterograde (ventricular) + retrograde (atrial) conduction</li><li>General rule: fastest PM controls heart</li><li>Mechanism: often unusual irritability of automatic PM cells in junctional tissue</li><li>Compensatory pause: overall timing not affected</li></ul>
Regularity	Irregular
Rate	Depends on underlying rhythm
Pw	<ul><li>None, antegrade, or retrograde</li><li>Abnormal axis (inverted in II, III, aVF; upright in aVR)</li></ul>
Pw:QRS ratio	None or 1:1 (if antegrade/retrograde Pw present)
PR interval	None, short, or retrograde (presence does not represent atrial stimulation of ventricles)
QRS interval	Normal (70-110 ms; similar to underlying rhythm)
Grouping	Often none, but possible (bigeminy, trigeminy)
Dropped beats	None

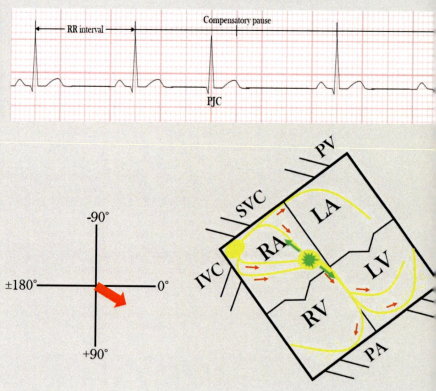

Junctional Escape Beat

Junctional Escape Beat	• Sinus node fails to fire → impulse originates w/in AV node → anterograde (ventricular) + retrograde (atrial) conduction → "resets" sinus node • Noncompensatory pause: overall timing affected
Regularity	Irregular
	Depends on underlying rhythm
	• None, antegrade, or retrograde • Abnormal axis (inverted in II, III, aVF; upright in aVR)
P:QRS ratio	None or 1:1 (if antegrade/retrograde Pw present)
PR interval	None, short, or retrograde (presence does not represent atrial stimulation of ventricles)
QRS interval	Normal (70-110 ms; similar to underlying rhythm)
Grouping	None
Dropped beats	Yes

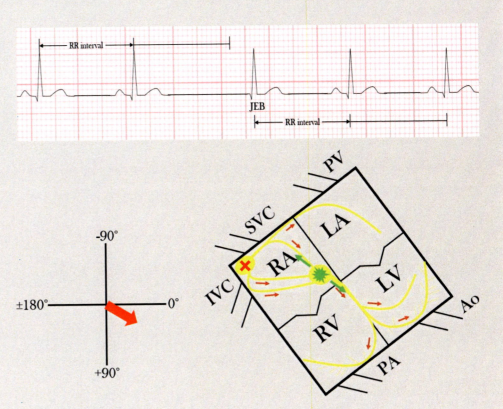

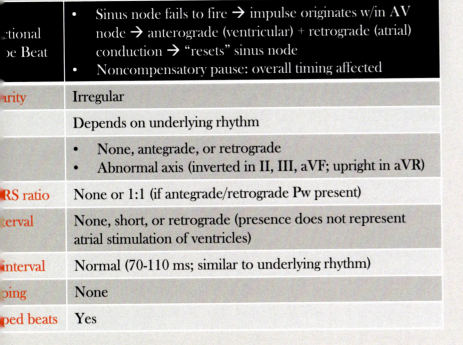

46.0

Junctional Escape Rhythm

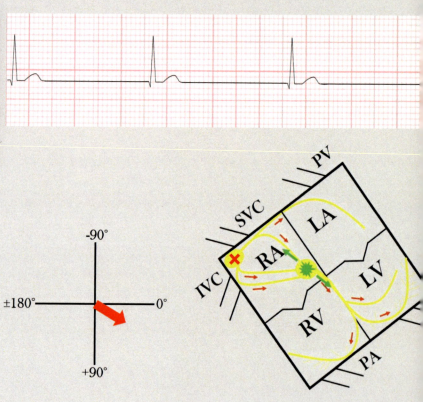

Junctional Escape Rhythm	<ul><li>Sinus node/atrial PMs fail to fire → impulse originates w/in AV junction → anterograde (ventricular) + retrograde (atrial) conduction</li><li>Causes: severe sinus bradycardia; sinus arrest; SA exit block; high-grade 2nd-/3rd-degree AVB; ↑ K; meds (βB, CCB, or digoxin toxicity)</li><li>Junctional rhythm terminology: based on HR ✓ <40 BPM = junctional bradycardia ✓ 40-60 BPM = junctional escape rhythm ✓ 60-100 BPM = accelerated junctional rhythm ✓ >100 BPM = junctional tachycardia</li></ul>
Regularity	Regular
Rate	40-60 BPM
Pw	• None, antegrade, or retrograde • Abnormal axis (inverted in II, III, aVF; upright in aVR)
Pw:QRS ratio	None or 1:1 (if antegrade/retrograde Pw present)
PR interval	None, short, or retrograde (not represent atrial stimulation of ventricles)
QRS interval	Normal (70-110 ms; similar to underlying rhythm)
Grouping	None
Dropped beats	None

Accelerated Junctional Rhythm

- Rapid impulses originate w/in AV junction (rate > sinus node) →
  anterograde (ventricular) + retrograde (atrial) conduction
- Mechanism: ↑ AVN + ↓ SA nodal automaticity (± sinus dysfunction)
- Causes: myocardial ischemia; myocarditis; cardiac surgery; meds
  (digoxin toxicity = classic; β-agonists = isoproterenol, epinephrine)
- Junctional rhythm terminology: based on HR
  - ✓ <40 BPM = junctional bradycardia
  - ✓ 40-60 BPM = junctional escape rhythm
  - ✓ 60-100 BPM = accelerated junctional rhythm
  - ✓ >100 BPM = junctional tachycardia

rity	Regular
	60-100 BPM
	• None, antegrade, or retrograde • Abnormal axis (inverted in II, III, aVF; upright in aVR)
RS ratio	None or 1:1 (if antegrade/retrograde Pw present)
erval	None, short, or retrograde (not represent atrial stimulation of ventricles)
nterval	Normal (70-110 ms; similar to underlying rhythm)
ing	None
ed beats	None

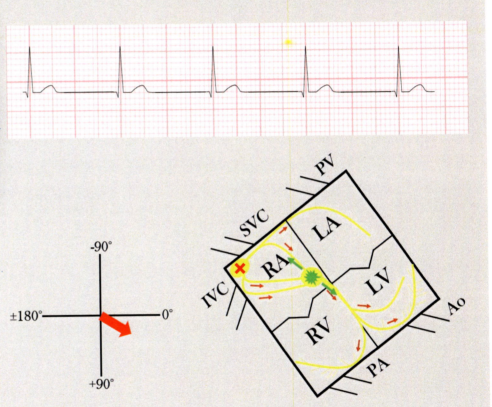

48.0

AV Nodal Reentrant Tachycardia

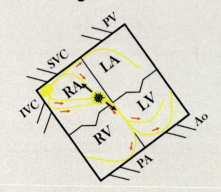

AV Nodal Reentrant Tachycardia (AVNRT)	<ul><li>SVT originating above His bundle; more prevalent in females</li><li>Causes: physical activity/exertion; coffee; tea; alcohol</li><li>Mechanism: reentry circuit w/in or around AVN; abrupt onset after PAC</li><li>3 main types: based on pathways & RP interval</li><li>1. Slow-fast (typical/common): slow antegrade + fast retrograde<ul><li>✓ ECG: Pw not visible, pseudo-Rw in V1, or pseudo-Sw in II, III, aVF</li></ul></li><li>2. Fast-slow (atypical/uncommon): fast antegrade + slow retrograde<ul><li>✓ ECG: Pw after QRS (QRS-P-T) in V1 or II (delayed atrial activation)</li></ul></li><li>3. Slow-slow: slow antegrade + slow retrograde<ul><li>✓ ECG: Pw before QRS in V1 or II</li></ul></li><li>Clinical significance: palpitations w/o structural HD (MCC); syncope; CP if CAD; SOB; anxiety; polyuria (↑ ANP); well-tolerated; rarely life-threatening</li><li>Management: vagal maneuvers (carotid sinus massage, Valsalva maneuvers); medications (adenosine, βBs, CCBs); cardioversion; catheter ablation</li></ul>
Regularity	Regular
Rate	140-280 BPM
Pw	(1) Slow-fast: often not visible; (2) fast-slow: after QRS; (3) slow-slow: before QRS
Pw:QRS ratio	None or 1:1 (if antegrade/retrograde Pw present)
PR interval	None, short, or retrograde (not represent atrial stimulation of ventricles)
QRS interval	Normal (70-110 ms)
Grouping	None
Dropped beats	None

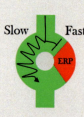

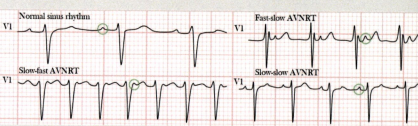

Wolff-Parkinson-White (WPW) Syndrome

- Ventricular preexcitation 2/2 to impulses bypassing AVN via AP (Kent bundle)
- WPW syndrome = congenital AP + characteristic ECG features + paroxysmal tachyarrhythmias (if no tachyarrhythmias = WPW pattern)
- Pathophysiology: 2 pathways b/t atria & ventricles
  - Pathway 1: AP (Kent bundle) b/t atria & ventricles → bypasses AVN → short PR interval + early ventricular depolarization (delta wave)
  - Pathway 2: normal AVN conduction
- Clinical significance: potentially life-threatening (small risk of SCD)
- Delta wave = slurring of initial QRS 2/2 ventricular preexcitation via AP
- ± discordant ST-Tw changes (directed opposite to main QRS vector)
- Pseudo-infarct pattern: negative delta waves (pseudo-Qw) in II, III, aVF/V2-V5 (mimics inferior/anterior MI); prominent Rw in V1-V3 (mimics posterior MI)

y	Regular in sinus rhythm
	60-100 BPM in sinus rhythm (+ episodic tachyarrhythmias)
	Present w/ constant morphology
ratio	1:1
val	Typically short (<120 ms)
erval	Prolonged (>110 ms; delta wave)
g	None
d beats	None

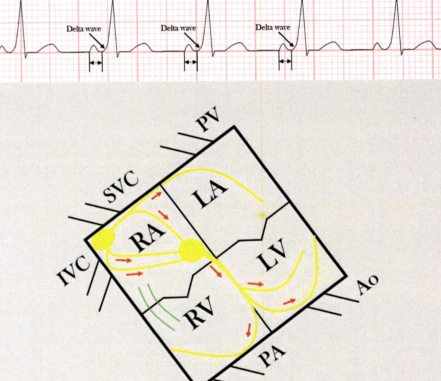

Lown-Ganong-Levine (LGL) Syndrome

Lown-Ganong-Levine (LGL) Syndrome	• Ventricular preexcitation 2/2 to impulses bypassing AVN via AP • James fibers (AP) bypass physiologic AVN delay → short PR interval • Clinical significance: typically benign ± tachyarrhythmias
Regularity	Regular
Rate	60-100 BPM in sinus rhythm
Pw	Present w/ constant morphology
Pw:QRS ratio	1:1
PR interval	Short (<120 ms)
QRS interval	Normal (70-110 ms; no delta wave)
Grouping	None
Dropped beats	None

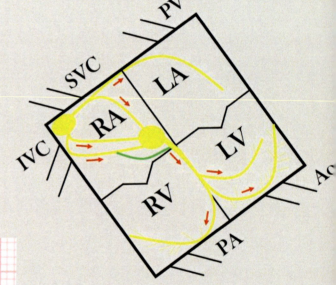

AV Reentrant Tachycardia

- AP allows for reentrant circuit to form b/t AP + AVN → AVRT
- Causes: congenital (eg, WPW) > surgically created
- AP conduction: both directions > retrograde (concealed) > antegrade
- Paroxysmal SVT w/ abrupt onset (PAC, PVC) & termination
- 2 types: based on direction of reentry conduction
    1. Orthodromic AVRT (MC): narrow QRS tachycardia
        - ✓ Antegrade conduction: AVN
        - ✓ Retrograde conduction: AP (concealed pathway)
        - ✓ Circuit: atria → <u>AVN</u> → ventricles → <u>AP</u>
    2. Antidromic AVRT: wide QRS tachycardia
        - ✓ Antegrade: AP
        - ✓ Retrograde: AVN
        - ✓ Circuit: atria → <u>AP</u> → ventricles → <u>AVN</u>

Regularity	Regular
Rate	200-300 BPM
P wave	Retrograde & inverted
P:QRS ratio	1:1
RP interval	Orthodromic AVRT (short RP interval) < antidromic AVRT
QRS interval	• Orthodromic AVRT: normal (70-110 ms) • Antidromic AVRT: prolonged (>110 ms; delta wave)
Grouping	None
Dropped beats	None

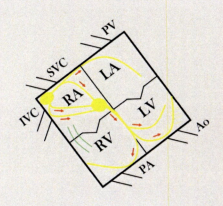

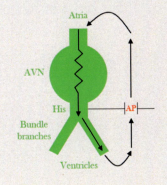

Orthodromic (narrow) AVRT

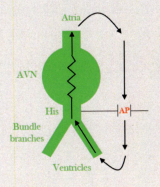

Antidromic (wide) AVRT

Premature Ventricular Contraction

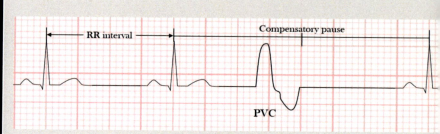

Premature Ventricular Contraction	<ul><li>Early beat originating from ectopic focus w/in ventricles</li><li>General rule: fastest PM controls heart</li><li>Mechanism: unusual irritability of automatic PM cells in ventricles</li><li>Causes: anxiety; myocardial ischemia; ↓ K; ↓ Mg; drugs (excess caffeine, β-agonists, sympathomimetics, digoxin toxicity)</li><li>Clinical significance: often benign (unless ↑ QT → torsades) & no tx required; ± palpitations; may trigger reentrant tachyarrhythmia</li><li>Compensatory pause: overall timing not affected</li><li>Discordant ST-Tw changes</li><li>Origin: RV (dominant Sw in V1); LV (dominant Rw in V1)</li></ul>
Regularity	Irregular
Rate	Depends on underlying rhythm
Pw	None or retrograde Pw (2/2 retrograde conduction)
Pw:QRS ratio	Often none (or 1:1 if retrograde Pw present)
PR interval	None
QRS interval	Prolonged (>110 ms) w/ abnormal QRS morphology
Grouping	None
Dropped beats	None

Terminology
- ✓ Unifocal (1 focus & morph) vs. multifocal (>1 foci & morph)
- ✓ Bigeminy (every 2nd); trigeminy (every 3rd); quadrigeminy (every 4th)
- ✓ Couplet (2 consecutive PVCs); triplet (3 consecutive PVCs)
- ✓ Frequent: >5/min (routine ECG) or >10-30/hr (ambulatory monitoring)

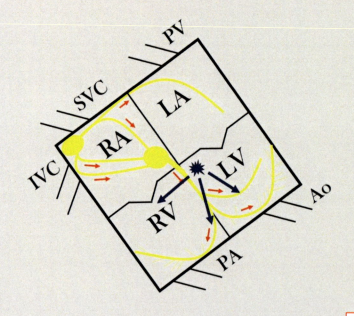

Ventricular Escape Beat

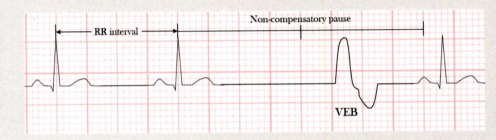

Ventricular Escape Beat	• Supraventricular PM cells fail to fire → impulse originates w/in ventricle → late, wide, bizarre-appearing QRS • Causes: sinus node dysfunction; AVB w/ inadequate JER • Noncompensatory pause: overall timing affected
Regularity	Irregular
Rate	Depends on underlying rhythm
P wave	Often none (or retrograde Pw 2/2 retrograde conduction)
P:QRS ratio	Often none (or 1:1 if retrograde Pw present)
PR interval	Often none (or retrograde)
QRS interval	Prolonged (>110 ms) w/ abnormal QRS morphology
Grouping	None
Dropped beats	None

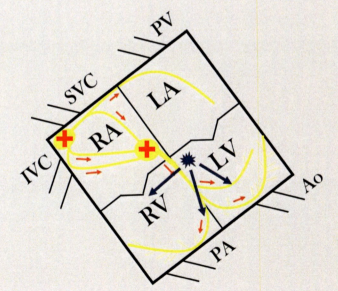

54.0

Ventricular Escape (Idioventricular) Rhythm

Ventricular Escape (Idioventricular) Rhythm	• Supraventricular PM cells fail to fire → impulses originate w/in ventricle → ventricular rhythm at <40 BPM • Isolated or component of 3rd-degree AVB/AV dissociation • Causes: severe sinus bradycardia; sinus arrest/dysfunction; SA exit block; AVB w/ inadequate JER; ↑ K; meds (βB, CCB, or digoxin toxicity)
Regularity	Regular
Rate	<40 BPM
Pw	Often none (or retrograde Pw 2/2 retrograde conduction)
Pw:QRS ratio	Often none (or 1:1 if retrograde Pw present)
PR interval	Often none (or retrograde)
QRS interval	Prolonged (>110 ms) w/ abnormal QRS morphology
Grouping	None
Dropped beats	None

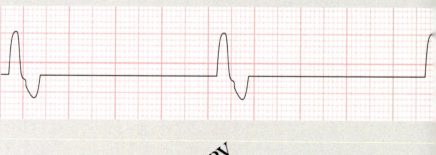

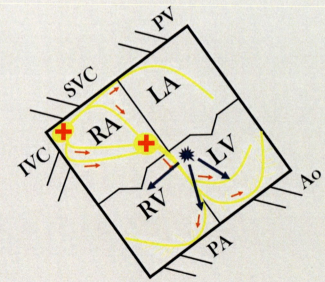

Accelerated Idioventricular Rhythm

- Ectopic ventricular **PM** fires faster than sinus node
- Often associated w/ ↑ vagal tone & ↓ sympathetic tone
- Mechanism: enhanced automaticity ± triggered activity (ischemia)
- Causes: reperfusion phase of acute STEMI (MCC); CM; CHD; myocarditis; ROSC post-cardiac arrest; athletic heart; anemia; ↓ K; drugs (β-agonists; digoxin, cocaine, opioid, or desflurane toxicity)
- Clinical significance: often well-tolerated, benign, self-limiting, & not require tx; correct underlying cause (eg, electrolytes, ischemia)
- Isorhythmic AV dissociation: sinus & ventricular complexes occur at same rate (Pw buried in QRS/Tw)
- ± fusion beats: sinus & ventricular beats coincide → hybrid QRS
- ± capture beats: sinus node "captures" ventricles → normal QRS

Accelerated ventricular Rhythm

Regularity	Regular
Rate	40-120 BPM
Pw	Often none (or retrograde Pw 2/2 retrograde conduction)
P:QRS ratio	Often none (or 1:1 if retrograde Pw present)
PR interval	Often none (or retrograde)
QRS interval	Prolonged (>110 ms; ≥3 wide QRS w/ abnormal morphology)
Grouping	None
Dropped beats	None

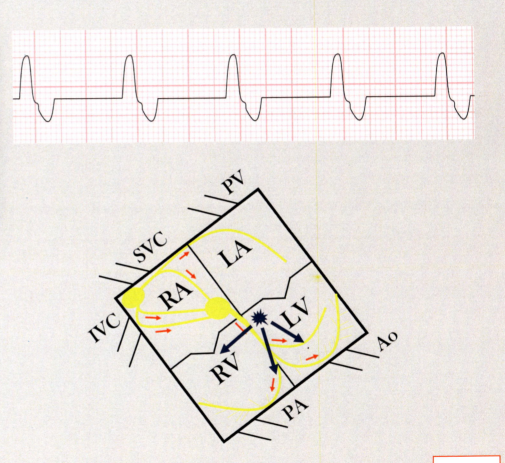

56.0

Fusion & Capture Beats

Key Points

- Assist in making diagnosis of V-Tach
- Fusion (Dressler) beat: sinus/supraventricular & ventricular beats coincide → hybrid QRS
- Capture beat: sinus node transiently "captures" ventricles in AV dissociation → normal QRS

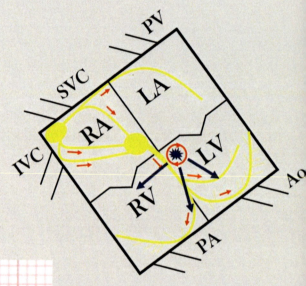

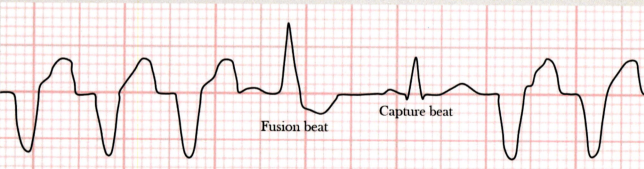

Brugada's & Josephson's Signs

Key Points

- Assist in making diagnosis of V-Tach
- Brugada's sign: QRS onset to Sw nadir >100 ms
- Josephson's sign: notching near nadir of Sw

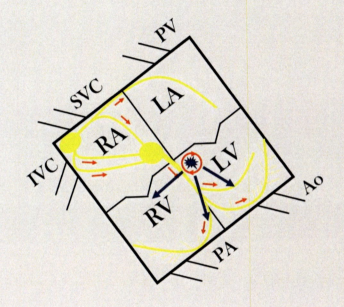

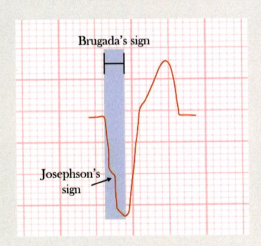

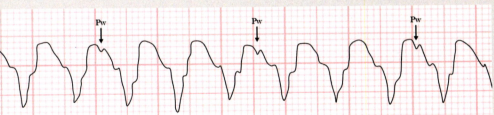

Ventricular Tachycardia

- Wide complex tachycardia originating from ectopic ventricular PM
- Ectopic ventricular PM fires faster than sinus node
- Classification: morph, duration (± sustained), presentation (± stable)
- Mechanism: reentry > triggered activity, enhanced automaticity
- Causes: ischemic HD; dilated/hypertrophic CM; Chaga's disease
- Clinical significance: impair CO → HoTN → collapse + acute HF + ↓ myocardial perfusion (→ V-Fib); immediate treatment required
- Abrupt onset & termination
- AV dissociation (± retrograde atrial conduction)
- ± fusion beats: sinus & ventricular beats coincide → hybrid QRS
- ± capture beats: sinus node "captures" ventricles → normal QRS
- Extreme QRS axis deviation (positive in aVR; negative in I & aVF)
- Complete positive/negative concordance in V1-V6
- Brugada's & Josephson's signs
- RSR' complexes in V1-V2 w/ R > R' amplitude

Regularity	Regular
Rate	120-200 BPM
Pw	Dissociated atrial rate
Pw:QRS ratio	Varies
PR interval	Often none (or retrograde)
QRS interval	Prolonged (≥160 ms; ≥3 wide QRS w/ abnormal morphology)
Grouping	None
Dropped beats	None

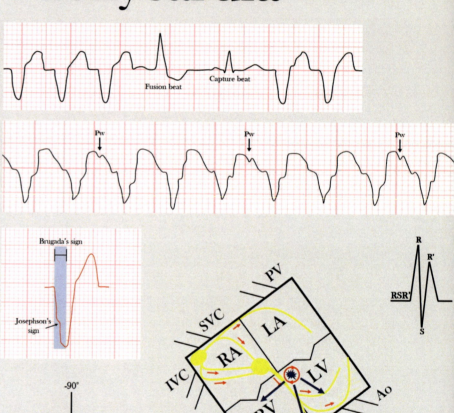

Reentrant Ventricular Tachycardia

Key Points

Reentry = most common mechanism of V-Tach

Occurs w/ unidirectional block 2/2 insult (occlusion)

General course of impulse:
1. Travels down 1 path (other path blocked)
2. Ventricular wall impulse bypasses block
3. Reentrant circuit forms

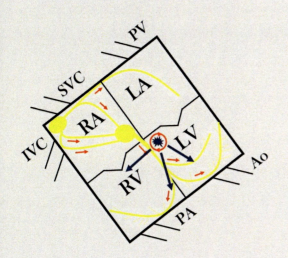

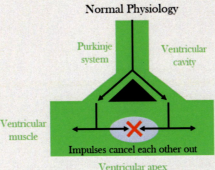

Normal Physiology
Purkinje system, Ventricular cavity, Ventricular muscle, Ventricular apex
Impulses cancel each other out

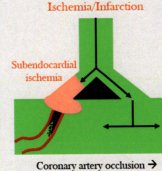

Ischemia/Infarction
Subendocardial ischemia
Coronary artery occlusion → subendocardial ischemia

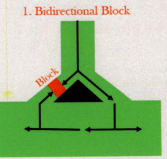

1. Bidirectional Block
Both weak impulse of Purkinje system & strong impulse of ventricular wall blocked by depressed region

2. Unidirectional Block

2A
Weak impulse of Purkinje system blocked by depressed region

2B
Strong impulse of ventricular wall bypasses depressed region

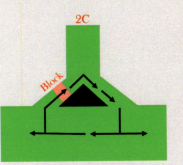

2C
Time to complete circuit less than refractory period → reentrant V-Tach

60.0

Torsades de Pointes

Torsades de Pointes (TdP)	· Form of polymorphic V-Tach occurring w/ prolonged QT interval
	· "Twisting of points": QRSs twist around isoelectric line
	· Undulating, sinusoidal appearance w/ QRS axis changing from positive to negative & back in haphazard fashion
	· Pathophysiology:
	  ✓ ↑ QT = prolonged repolarization 2/2 ion channel dysfunction → early after-depolarizations (tall Uw or PVC)
	  ✓ "R-on-T" phenomenon (PVC occurs during Tw) → TdP
	  ✓ "Pause-dependent" TdP: preceded by short-long-short RR intervals; longer pauses associated w/ faster runs of TdP
	· Causes: electrolyte disturbances (↓ K); channelopathies (long QT syndrome); meds (macrolides, TCAs, antipsychotics, chloroquine, antidepressants, antihistamines, IA/IC/III antiarrhythmics, etc.)
	· Clinical significance: often short-lived & self-terminating; ± hemodynamic instability/collapse; may convert into NSR or V-Fib

Regularity	Irregular
Rate	200-250 BPM
Pw	None
Pw:QRS ratio	None
PR interval	None
QRS interval	Variable
Grouping	Variable sinusoidal pattern
Dropped beats	None

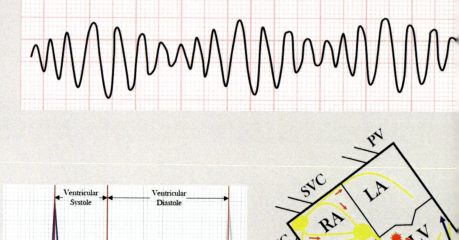

Helpful Tips
✓ "Twisting" morphology may not be seen during short runs or single-lead recording
✓ TdP >220 BPM = longer duration + ↑ risk of degenerating into V-Fib
✓ Abnormal ("giant") T-U waves may precede TdP (esp. in long QT syndrome)
✓ Bigeminy PVCs (every other) in long QT syndrome may be clue of imminent TdP

Ventricular Flutter

Ventricular Flutter	• Extreme form of V-Tach w/ loss of organized electrical activity • Sinusoidal pattern w/ no discernible components • If ≥300 BPM: ? WPW syndrome w/ 1:1 AV conduction of A-Flut • Clinical significance: rapid, significant hemodynamic compromise; progresses to V-Fib; immediate advanced life support required
Regularity	Regular
Rate	>200 BPM
P wave	None
P:QRS ratio	None
PR interval	None
QRS interval	Prolonged (>110 ms) w/ abnormal morphology (sinusoidal pattern)
Grouping	None
Dropped beats	None

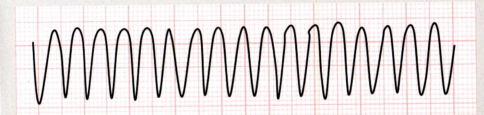

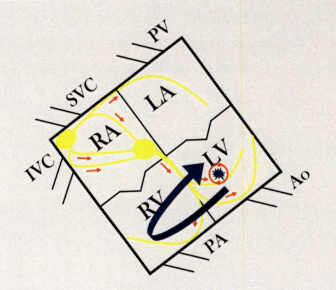

62.0

Ventricular Fibrillation

Ventricular Fibrillation	• Chaotic ventricular depolarization → no synchronized ventricular contractions → no cardiac output → SCD w/o advanced life support • Irregular deflections of varying amplitude w/o discernible waveforms • Prolonged V-Fib → progressive ↓ energy stores → ↓ waveform amplitude (ie, coarse V-Fib ≥3 mm → fine V-Fib <3 mm → asystole) • Mechanism: not fully understood (multiple wavelet vs. mother rotors) • Causes: myocardial ischemia/infarction; CM; channelopathies; aortic stenosis/dissection; myocarditis; cardiac tamponade; blunt trauma; tension PTX; pulm embolism; ↑ QT → R-on-T → TdP; ↓ T; sepsis • Clinical significance: fatal w/o immediate advanced life support
Regularity	Chaotic irregular rhythm
Rate	150-500 BPM or indeterminate
Pw	None
Pw:QRS ratio	None
PR interval	None
QRS interval	None
Grouping	None
Dropped beats	No beats present

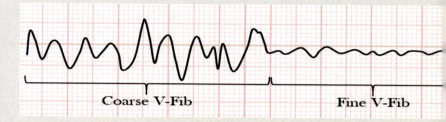

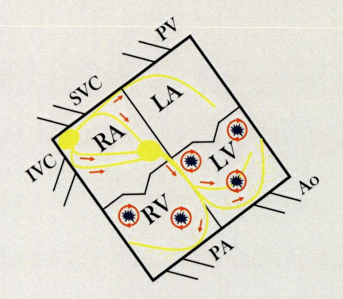

Asystole

Asystole	• No electrical heart activity (ie, no ventricular contractions → no blood flow to rest of body) • No atrial/ventricular depolarizations; often irreversible • ECG: no rhythm, waveforms, or rate (cardiac flatline) • Brady-asystole: asystole + occasional QRSs • Management: ACLS protocol
arity	None
	None
	None
QRS ratio	None
interval	None
interval	None
ping	None
ped beats	None

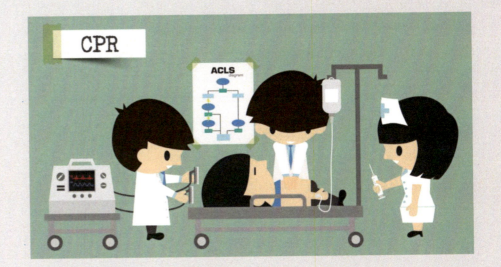

64.0

Pulseless Electrical Activity

Key Points

- PEA: absent cardiac contractions + coordinated electrical activity (ie, electromechanical dissociation)
    - ECG: any waveform w/o a pulse
    - Reversible causes: "Hs & Ts"
        - <u>H</u>yperkalemia, <u>H</u>ypoxia, <u>H</u>ypothermia, <u>H</u>ydrogen ion excess (acidosis), <u>H</u>ypovolemia, <u>H</u>ypoglycemia
        - <u>T</u>amponade (cardiac), <u>T</u>ension pneumothorax, <u>T</u>hrombosis (PE, MI), <u>T</u>oxins (overdose), <u>T</u>rauma
    - Management: ACLS protocol + correct underlying cause
    - Prognosis: often poor

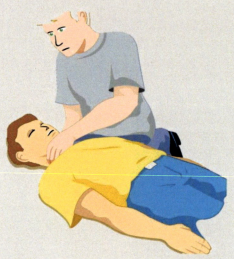

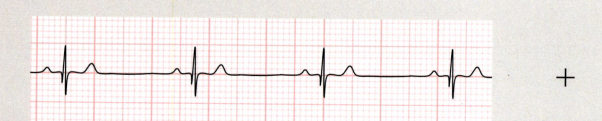 +

Pacemaker Rhythms

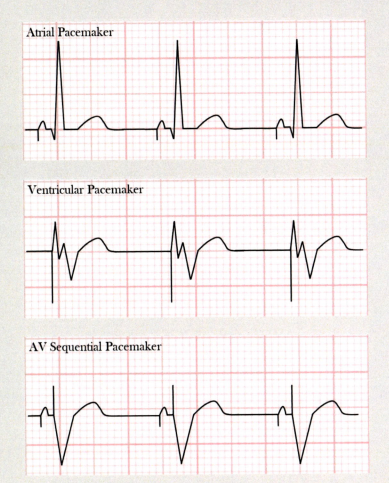
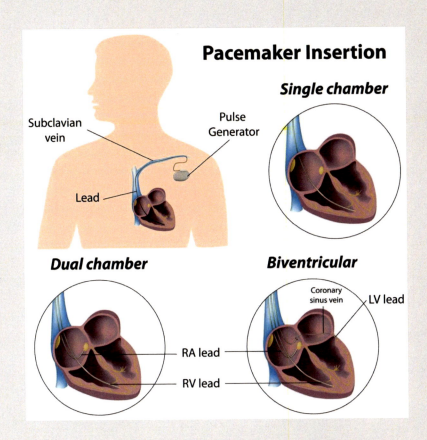

Part III: Chamber Enlargement

TOPICS:

Atrial Enlargement
★ 67.0 Right Atrial Enlargement
★ 68.0 Left Atrial Enlargement
   69.0 Biatrial Enlargement

Ventricular Hypertrophy
   70.0 Right Ventricular Hypertrophy
★ 71.0 Left Ventricular Hypertrophy
   72.0 Biventricular Hypertrophy

★ High-Yield Topic

Right Atrial Enlargement

Key Points

- Pw = atrial depolarization (RA → LA)
  - ✓ Initial Pw: directed anteriorly
  - ✓ Terminal Pw: directed posteriorly
- RAE: ↑ Pw amplitude; ≥1 of the following
  - ✓ II, III, aVF: ≥2.5 mm (P-pulmonale)
  - ✓ V1-V2: initial positive deflection ≥1.5 mm
- Causes: pHTN 2/2 chronic lung dz, tricuspid stenosis, 1° pHTN, CHD (pulm stenosis, ToF)

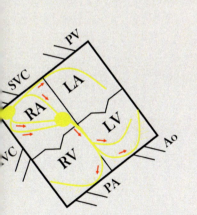
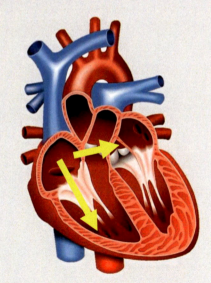
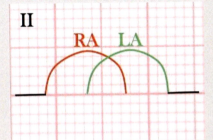
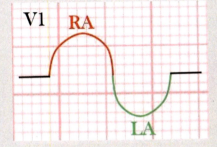
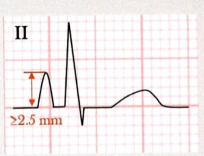
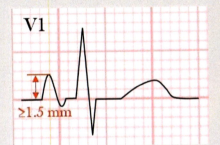

Left Atrial Enlargement

Key Points

- Pw = atrial depolarization (RA → LA)
  - ✓ Initial Pw: directed anteriorly
  - ✓ Terminal Pw: directed posteriorly
- LAE: ↑ Pw duration ± depth; often precursor to A-Fib
  - ✓ V1 (terminal negative deflection):
    - [depth (mm)] x [duration (s)] ≥ −0.04 mm·s
    - Ex: [≥ −1 mm depth] x [≥ 0.04 s duration]
  - ✓ II (P-mitrale): "M-shaped" Pw
    - [notched Pw w/ inter-peak duration ≥ 40 ms] + [total Pw duration > 110 ms]
- Causes: MS if isolated; HTN, AS, MR, or HCM if assoc. LVH

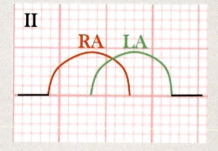
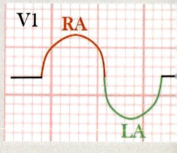
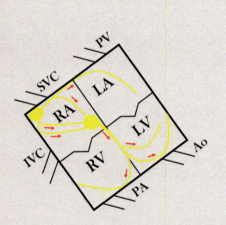
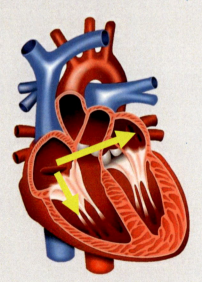
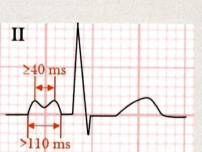
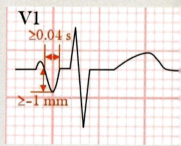

Biatrial Enlargement

Key Points

BAE = RAE + LAE criteria met

RAE: ↑ Pw amplitude; ≥1 of the following
- ✓ II: ≥2.5 mm (P-pulmonale)
- ✓ V1 (initial positive deflection): ≥1.5 mm

LAE: ↑ Pw duration ± depth
- ✓ II (P-mitrale): [notched Pw w/ inter-peak duration ≥40 ms] + [total Pw duration >110 ms]
- ✓ V1 (terminal negative deflection): [depth (mm)] x [duration (s)] ≥ -0.04 mm·s

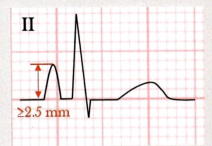

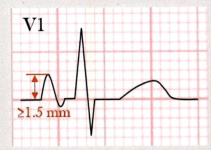

RAE

+

LAE

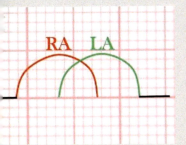

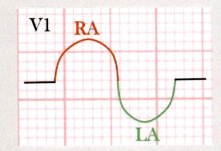

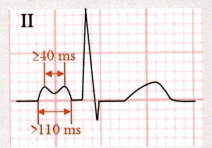

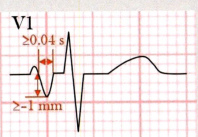

Right Ventricular Hypertrophy

Key Points

- RVH → ↑ anterior & rightward forces
- ECG criteria:
  - ✓ RAD (>+110°)
  - ✓ Dominant Rw in V1-V2 (>7 mm tall or R > S)
  - ✓ Dominant Sw in V5-V6 (>7 mm deep or R < S)
  - ✓ QRS duration <120 ms (changes not from RBBB)
  - ✓ *Note: RVH can cause incomplete/complete RBBB (if present, voltage criteria does not apply)
- Supporting evidence of RVH:
  - ✓ RAE (P-pulmonale: ↑ Pw amplitude in II/V1)
  - ✓ RV strain pattern: STD/TWI in V1-V4, II, III, aVF
  - ✓ $S_1S_2S_3$ pattern (RAD w/ S ≥ R in I, II, III)
  - ✓ Deep Sw in I, aVL, V5-V6
  - ✓ ↑ Rw peak time (35-55 ms) in V1-V2
- Causes: pHTN; MS; chronic lung disease; pulmonary embolism; CHD (pulmonary stenosis, ToF); ARVD

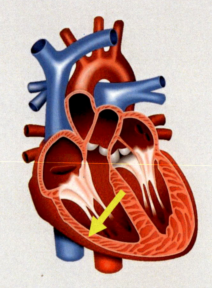

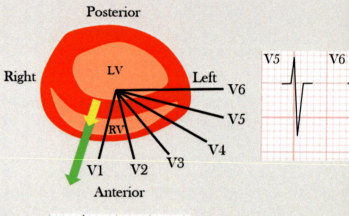

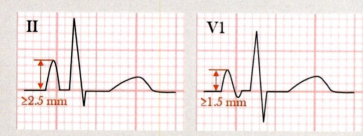

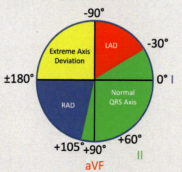

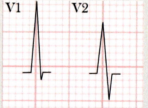

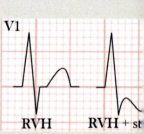

Left Ventricular Hypertrophy

Key Points

- LVH → ↑ posterior & left-lateral forces
- ✓ ECG diagnosis requires voltage + non-voltage criteria

Voltage criteria:
- ✓ Limb leads:
  - [R (I)] + [S (III)] >25 mm
  - R: I >14 mm; aVL ≥11-12 mm; aVF >20-21 mm
  - S (aVR) >14-15 mm
- ✓ Precordial leads:
  - [S (V1 or V2)] + [R (V5 or V6)] ≥35 mm
  - R (V4, V5, or V6) >26 mm
  - R: V5 >26 mm; V6 >20 mm
  - [largest R] + [largest S] >45 mm

Non-voltage criteria:
- ✓ ↑ Rw peak time (≥45 ms) in V5-V6 ± slight ↑ QRS duration (2/2 ↑ myocardial mass)
- ✓ Secondary ST-T changes (LV strain pattern):
  - Downsloping STD + asymmetric TWI in V4-V6
  - Concave STE + asymmetric upright Tw in V1-V3

Supporting evidence of LVH:
- ✓ LAE (P-mitrale)
- ✓ LAD (-30° to -90°)
- ✓ Prominent Uw (proportional to ↑ QRS amplitude)

Causes: HTN; AS; AR; MR; coarctation of the aorta; HCM

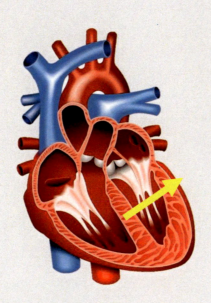
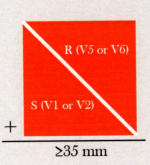
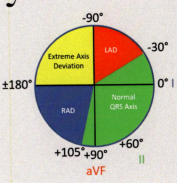
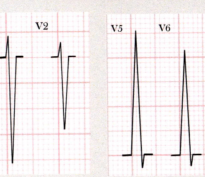
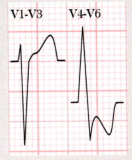

Factors influencing QRS amplitude:
- ✓ ↑ distance b/t heart & electrodes (obesity, COPD) → ↓ amplitude
- ✓ ↑ age → ↓ amplitude
- ✓ Sex: females < males
- ✓ Athletes → ↑ amplitude (2/2 ventricular remodeling)

71.0

Biventricular Hypertrophy

Key Points

- BVH = RVH + LVH
  - ECG: low sensitivity for detecting; possibly normal 2/2 partial cancellation of RVH & LVH forces
- ECG criteria: LVH criteria + ...
  - RAD (>+110°)
  - V5 or V6: deep Sw (>6 mm)
  - Multiple leads w/ large RS complexes
  - P-pulmonale (↑ Pw amplitude in II/V1; sign of RAE)
  - Katz-Wachtel phenomenon: tall biphasic QRS in V2-V5

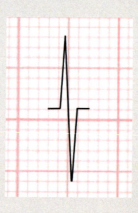

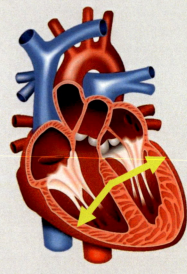

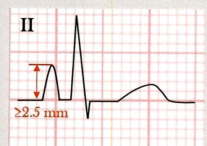

II
≥2.5 mm

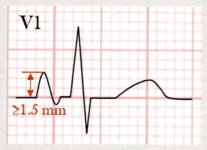

V1
≥1.5 mm

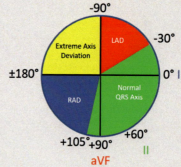

Part IV: Conduction Defects

TOPICS:

AV Blocks

1.0 First-Degree AV Block
2.0 Second-Degree AV Block Mobitz I (Wenckebach)
3.0 Second-Degree AV Block Mobitz II
4.0 Third-Degree (Complete) AV Block
5.0 AV Dissociation

Intraventricular Conduction Defects

6.0 Right Bundle Branch Block
7.0 Left Bundle Branch Block
8.0 Left Anterior Fascicular Block
9.0 Left Posterior Fascicular Block
10.0 Bifascicular Block
11.0 Nonspecific Intraventricular Conduction Delay

EKG.MD

High-Yield Topic

First-Degree AV Block

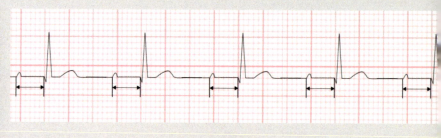

First-Degree AV Block	• Minor AV conduction defect: partial block at/below AVN • Pw always precede QRS, but fixed, prolonged PR interval (atrial activation transmitted to ventricles w/ constant delay) • Causes: normal variant; ↑ vagal tone (athlete); inferior MI; MV surgery; myocarditis (Lyme disease); ↑ K; AV nodal blocking agents (βBs, CCBs, digoxin, amiodarone) • Clinical significance: not cause hemodynamic instability; no specific treatment typically required
Regularity	Regular
Rate	Depends on underlying rhythm
Pw	Present w/ same morphology & axis
Pw:QRS ratio	1:1
PR interval	Constant, prolonged (>200 ms; "marked" = >300 ms)
QRS interval	Normal (70-110 ms)
Grouping	None
Dropped beats	None

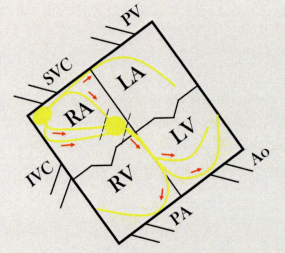

Second-Degree AV Block Mobitz I (Wenckebach)

- Progressive PR interval lengthening w/ intermittent dropped beats
  - ✓ "Longer-longer-longer-drop, that's a sign of Wenckebach"
- Reversible conduction block at AVN crest or A-AVN junction
- Malfunctioning AVN cells progressively fatigue until failing to conduct an impulse (ie, injured AVN w/ long refractory period)
- Causes: ↑ vagal tone (athletes); inferior MI; myocarditis (Lyme disease); MV repair; meds (βBs, CCBs, digoxin, amiodarone)
- Clinical significance: often benign ± minimal hemodynamic instability; low risk of progressing to 3rd-degree AVB
  - ✓ Asymptomatic: no treatment generally required
  - ✓ Symptomatic: atropine; rarely require permanent pacing

ularity	Regularly irregular
e	Depends on underlying rhythm
	Present w/ same morphology & axis; relatively constant PP interval
QRS ratio	Varies (2:1, 3:2, 4:3, 5:4, etc.)
interval	• Progressively lengthens until non-conducted Pw (dropped beat) • Longest/shortest PR interval immediately before/after dropped beat • PR interval after dropped beat shorter than before dropped beat • Greatest ↑ in PR interval often b/t 1st & 2nd beats of cycle
S interval	Normal (70–110 ms)
uping	Yes & varies
pped beats	Yes

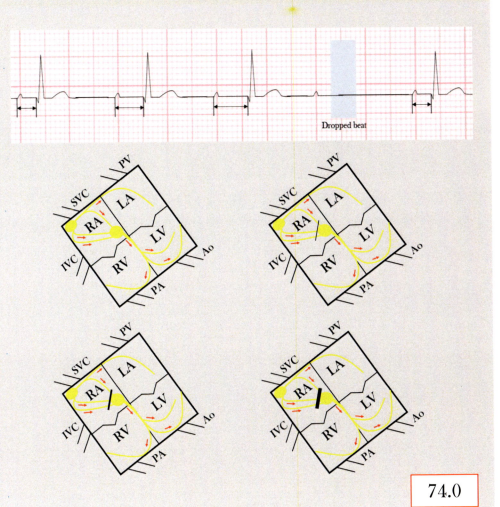

74.0

Second-Degree AV Block Mobitz II

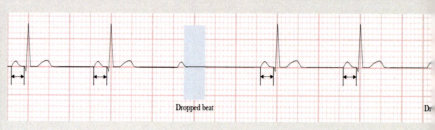

Dropped beat

Second-Degree AVB Mobitz II	• Intermittent dropped QRS (non-conducted Pw) w/o prior PR interval lengthening (normal, constant PR when conducted) • Conduction failure at His-Purkinje system (ie, below AVN) • Causes: anterior MI; idiopathic conduction system fibrosis; MV repair; myocarditis; Lyme disease; rheumatic HD; amyloidosis; SLE; sarcoidosis; ↑ K; meds (βBs, CCBs, digoxin, amiodarone) • Clinical significance: risk of hemodynamic compromise, severe bradycardia, & progressing to complete AVB; permanent PM
Regularity	Regularly irregular
Rate	Depends on underlying rhythm
Pw	Present w/ same morphology & axis
Pw:QRS ratio	Varies ([X:X−1] → 3:2, 4:3, 5:4, etc., or no pattern)
PR interval	Normal (120-200 ms) & constant
QRS interval	• Normal (70-110 ms) if block w/in His bundle • Prolonged (>110 ms) if block below His bundle
Grouping	Yes & varies
Dropped beats	Yes

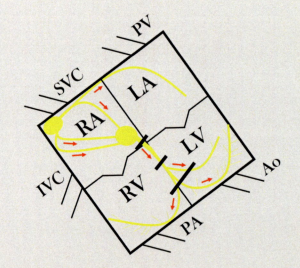

Third-Degree (Complete) AV Block

- Complete absence of AVN conduction (ie, no supraventricular impulses conducted to ventricles)
- No relationship b/t Pw & QRS (ie, AV dissociation)
- End point of 2nd-degree AVB Mobitz I & II
- Conduction failure above (Mobitz I) or below (Mobitz II) AVN
- Causes: inferior/anterior MI; idiopathic conduction system fibrosis; Lyme disease; meds (βBs, CCBs, digoxin, amiodarone)
- Clinical significance: high risk of hemodynamic compromise, ventricular tachycardia/standstill, & SCD; requires permanent PM

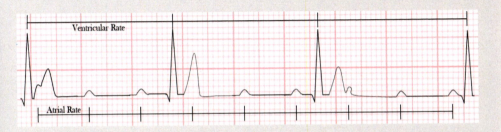

arity	Regular, but independent atrial & ventricular intervals
	Independent; atrial (Pw) > ventricular (QRS; depends on escape rhythm)
	Present w/ same morphology & axis
RS ratio	Varies (Pw > QRS)
terval	Varies; no pattern
interval	- Normal (70-110 ms) if block <u>above</u> AVN (JER at 40-60 BPM) - Prolonged (>110 ms) if block <u>below</u> AVN (VER at <40 BPM)
ping	None
ped beats	None

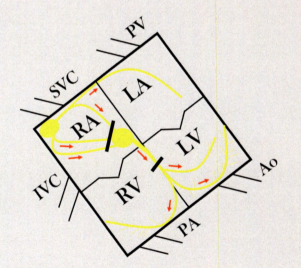

76.0

AV Dissociation

AV Dissociation	• Atria & ventricles under control of separate PMs & beat independently (no antegrade or retrograde conduction) • No relationship b/t Pw & QRS w/ ventricular rate > atrial rate • Causes: sinoatrial block; complete AVB; unusual ventricular irritability ("interference dissociation") 2/2 AIVR, V-Tach) • Isorhythmic AV dissociation: sinus & ventricular complexes occur at same rate (Pw buried in QRS/Tw)
Regularity	Regular, but independent atrial & ventricular intervals
Rate	Independent; atrial (Pw) < ventricular (QRS)
Pw	Present w/ same morphology & axis (± distorted if overlaps)
Pw:QRS ratio	Varies (Pw < QRS)
PR interval	Not measurable (no pattern)
QRS interval	• Normal (70-110 ms) if junctional escape focus • Prolonged (>110 ms) if ventricular escape focus
Grouping	None
Dropped beats	None

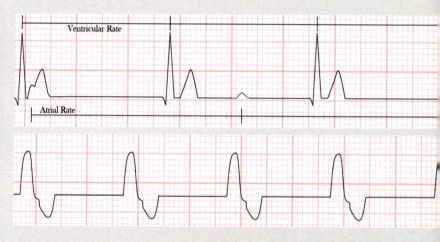

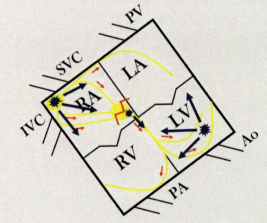

Right Bundle Branch Block

Key Points
- RBBB: anatomical/functional dysfunction in RBB
  - Block causes impulse to travel down unobstructed LBB 1st → slow cell-to-cell depolarization from L-to-R → [± wide QRS] + [new R' in V1-V2] + [slurred Sw in V5-V6, I, aVL]
- ECG criteria:
  - QRS interval ≥120 ms (complete); <120 ms (incomplete)
  - V1-V2: rsr', rsR', or rSR' pattern ("M" or "rabbit ears"; Sw may not always reach baseline; R' > R)
    - QR' pattern if anteroseptal MI
  - V5-V6, I, aVL: Sw > Rw duration by ≥40 ms (slurred Sw)
  - ST-Tw discordant to main QRS vector (concordance may suggest underlying pathology – eg, myocardial ischemia)
- Causes: idiopathic RBB fibrosis/degeneration; CHD (ASD); IHD (LAD); acute cor pulmonale (PE); COPD; RVH; HCM; cardiac surgery (transient/permanent RBBB); PCI (transient RBBB)
- Clinical significance: not correlated w/ adverse outcomes if asymptomatic; new RBBB + CP → ± LAD occlusion; new RBBB + SOB → ± PE; ischemia/MI dx not affected, but limits RVH dx

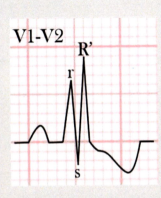
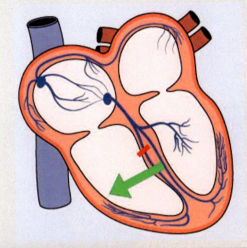
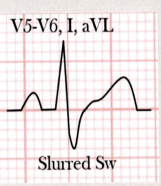
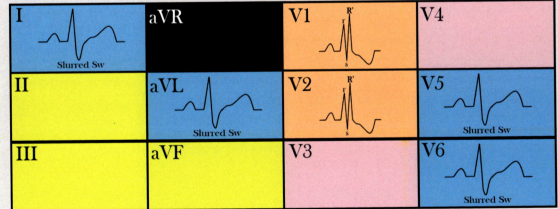

78.0

Left Bundle Branch Block

Key Points

- LBBB: anatomical/functional dysfunction in LBB or [LAF + LPF]
  - Block causes impulse to travel down unobstructed RBB 1st → slow cell-to-cell depolarization from R-to-L → [± wide QRS] + [broad Sw in V1-V2] + [broad Rw V5-V6, I, aVL]
- ECG criteria:
  - QRS interval ≥120 ms (complete); <120 ms (incomplete)
  - V1-V2: deep, broad Sw (± notching; "W") ± small Rw
  - V5-V6, I, aVL: broad, monophasic Rw (no Qw except aVL)
  - ST-Tw discordant to main QRS vector (concordance may suggest underlying pathology – eg, myocardial ischemia)
  - Other features: LAD; poor Rw progression in V1-V6; ↑ Rw peak time ≥45 ms in V5-V6
- Causes: idiopathic LBB fibrosis/degeneration; AS; HTN; IHD; HF; LVH; valvular dz; CM; anterior MI; myocarditis; digoxin toxicity; ↑ K
- Clinical significance: always pathological; adverse CV outcomes 2/2 impaired LV function; acquired LBBB → ↑ risk of HF, CAD, RVH; ischemia/MI dx affected (use Sgarbossa criteria); limits LVH dx

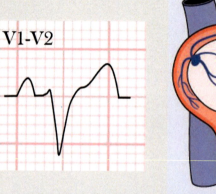
V1-V2

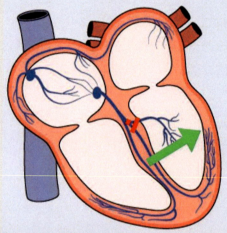

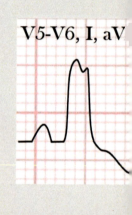
V5-V6, I, aV

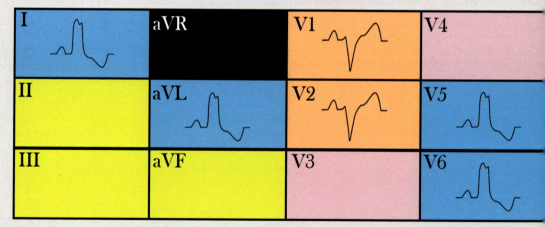

Left Anterior Fascicular Block

Key Points

LAFB (LAH): anatomical or functional dysfunction in LAF → LV depolarization depends on LPF
- LAF: thin, organized fibers innervating antero-lateral LV
- Vector 1: weaker + rightward & inferiorly-directed → [small Rw in II, III, aVF] + [small Qw in I, aVL]
- Vector 2: stronger + leftward & superiorly-directed → [deep Sw in II, III, aVF] + [large Rw in I, aVL] + LAD
- Vectors 1 + 2 → [rS in II, III, aVF] + [qR in I, aVL] + LAD

ECG criteria:
- LAD: -45° to -90° ("probable LAFB" if -30° to -45°)
- I, aVL: qR complexes (possible monophasic Rw in I)
- II, III, aVF: rS complexes
- QRS interval: <110 ms (± slightly prolonged by 10-40 ms)
- Other features: ↑ Rw peak time in aVL (>45 ms); ↑ QRS voltage in limb leads (± LVH voltage criteria, but no LV strain pattern)

Note: may mimic anteroseptal MI or mask inferior MI; TWI in I & aVL may mimic post-ischemic Tw

Causes: possible in healthy individuals, but most w/ significant HD; HTN; LVH; CAD; MI; dilated/hypertrophic CM; degenerative disease; myocarditis; amyloidosis; ↑ K

Clinical significance: MC than LPFB (due to smaller arterial supply + thin bundle of fibers); isolated LAFB considered benign; some cases may progress to bifascicular block (LAFB + RBBB) or complete AVB

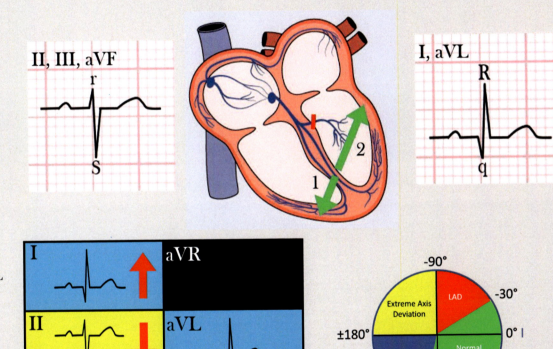

80.0

Left Posterior Fascicular Block

Key Points

- LPFB (LPH): anatomical or functional dysfunction in LPF → LV depolarization depends on LAF
    - ✓ LPF: dispersed, non-organized fibers innervating infero-posterior LV
    - ✓ Vector 1: weaker + leftward & superiorly-directed → [small Rw in I, aVL] + [small Qw in II, III, aVF]
    - ✓ Vector 2: stronger + rightward & inferiorly-directed → [deep Sw in I, aVL] + [large Rw in II, III, aVF] + RAD
    - ✓ Vectors 1 + 2 → [rS in I, aVL] + [qR in II, III, aVF] + RAD

- ECG criteria:
    - ✓ RAD (+90° to +180°)
    - ✓ I, aVL: rS complexes
    - ✓ II, III, aVF: qR complexes (requires small Qw in III & aVF)
    - ✓ QRS interval: <110 ms (± slightly prolonged by 10-40 ms)
    - ✓ Exclude other RAD causes (RVH, PE, TCA overdose, lateral MI)
    - ✓ Other features: ↑ Rw peak time in aVF (>45 ms); ↑ QRS voltage in limb leads (± LVH voltage criteria, but no LV strain pattern)

  *Note: may mimic inferior MI or mask lateral MI; TWI in II, III, & aVF may mimic post-ischemic Tw

- Clinical significance: less common than LAFB (due to larger arterial supply + dispersed fibers); rare in isolation (often occurs w/ RBBB)

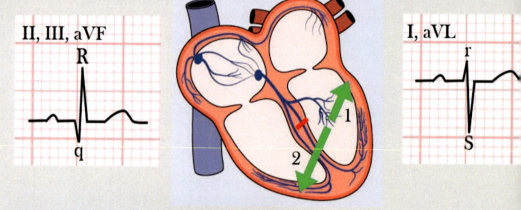

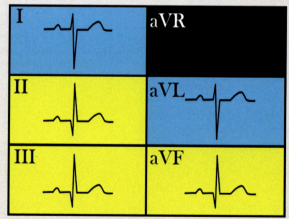

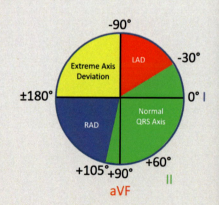

Bifascicular Block

Key Points

Bifascicular block: anatomical/functional dysfunction in [RBBB] + [LAFB or LPFB]
- ✓ Prevalence: [RBBB + LAFB] > [RBBB + LPFB]

RBBB + LAFB ECG criteria:
- ✓ QRS interval ≥120 ms
- ✓ V1-V2: rsr', rsR', or rSR' pattern (R' > R)
- ✓ V5-V6, I, aVL: slurred, wide Sw
- ✓ LAD
- ✓ I, aVL: qR complexes
- ✓ II, III, aVF: rS complexes

RBBB + LPFB ECG criteria:
- ✓ QRS interval ≥120 ms
- ✓ V1-V2: rsr', rsR', or rSR' pattern (R' > R)
- ✓ V5-V6, I, aVL: wide, slurred Sw
- ✓ RAD
- ✓ I, aVL: rS complexes
- ✓ II, III, aVF: qR complexes
- ✓ Exclude other causes of RAD (RVH, acute PE, TCA overdose, lateral MI)

Causes: ischemic HD (#1); degenerative disease of conduction system; HTN; aortic stenosis; anterior MI; congenital HD; ↑ K (may resolve if corrected)

Clinical significance: relatively low risk of progression to complete heart block
- ✓ RBBB + LAFB: common & stable pattern, except if new-onset w/ ischemia
- ✓ RBBB + LPFB: more common than isolated LPFB; unstable acute pattern may deteriorate into complete heart block (esp. w/ acute anterior MI)

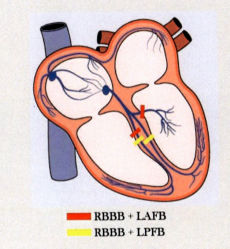

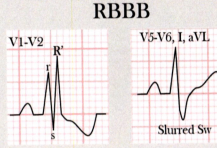

RBBB

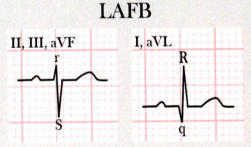

LAFB

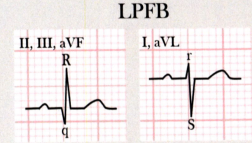

LPFB

Nonspecific Intraventricular Conduction Delay

Key Points

- Nonspecific IVCD ECG criteria:
  - ✓ QRS interval >110 ms (adults), >90 ms (8-16 y/o), >80 ms (<8 y/o)
  - ✓ Criteria for **RBBB** or **LBBB** not met

- Causes: normal variant; post-MI; myocardial fibrosis; amyloidosis; dilated CM; ventricular hypertrophy; WPW syndrome; PM-stimulated beats; Brugada syndrome; ARVD; electrolytes (↑ K); meds (TCA overdose)

- Clinical significance: ↑ risk of all-cause & CV mortality (esp. arrhythmia-associated deaths); consider other causes of wide QRS (see above)

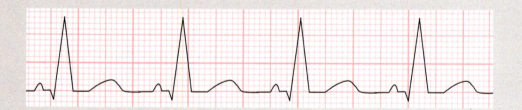

Part V: Myocardial Ischemia & Infarction

TOPICS:

- Ischemic Heart Disease
- Acute Myocardial Infarction
- ECG Classification of Ischemic Heart Disease
- ECG Basics in Myocardial Ischemia & Infarction
- ST-T Basics in Acute Myocardial Ischemia
- Injury Currents: Transmural vs. Subendocardial Ischemia
- ECG Progression in Acute Myocardial Ischemia
- ST Elevation & Depression in Acute Myocardia Ischemia
- T-Wave Changes in Acute Myocardial Ischemia
- Wellen's Syndrome
- de Winter's Sign
- T-Wave Pseudonormalization
- Pathological Q- & R-Waves

★ 97.0 Coronary Artery Anatomy & Dominance
★ 98.0 Left Ventricular Anatomy & Vascular Supply
★ 99.0 Localizing Ischemia in STEMI
★ 100.0 Right Coronary Artery Occlusion
★ 101.0 Left Anterior Descending Artery Occlusion
★ 102.0 Left Circumflex Artery Occlusion
★ 103.0 Left Main Coronary Artery Occlusion
★ 104.0 Prinzmetal's (Variant) Angina
105.0 Conduction System Vascular Supply
106.0 Conduction Defects in Myocardial Ischemia & Infarction
107.0 Sgarbossa Criteria
108.0 Conduction Defects in Inferior Wall MI
109.0 Conduction Defects in Anterior Wall MI

★ High-Yield Topic

Ischemic Heart Disease

Key Points

- CAD (equivalent to IHD) = #1 form of CVD & #1 killer worldwide
  - Due to atherosclerosis (lipid deposition) + inflammation
  - More aggressive if ↑ inflammation + ↑ CV risk factors
  - ↑ plaque size → ↑ stenosis (narrowing) → ↓ arterial blood flow
- Acute coronary syndrome (ACS):
  - Atherosclerosis + inflammation → plaque destabilization → rupture/erosion of endothelial covering → thrombogenic factor activation → thrombus formation (atherothrombosis) → arterial lumen obstruction → ↓ blood flow → myocardial ischemia
- ↑ cardiac workload → ↑ ATP requirement → ↑ O_2 demand
  - Stenosis → ↓ O_2 supply → supply-demand mismatch → myocardial ischemia (angina pectoris; reversible)
  - If perfusion not restored → infarction (necrosis; irreversible)
  - ↑ ischemic/infarct size → ↑ risk of HF, arrhythmias, complications

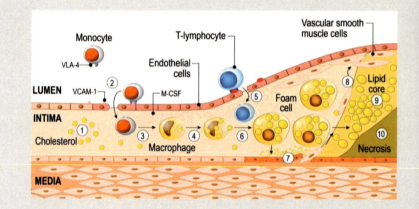

Healthy coronary artery

Plaque formation

Thrombosis

Acute Myocardial Infarction

Key Points

- AMI: most severe complication of CAD; perfusion not restored w/in 30 min of ischemia → infarction
  - Diagnostic criteria:
    1. ↑ cardiac troponins (required)
    2. Ischemic ECG changes (ST-T changes ± QRS changes)
    3. Symptoms (eg, CP, SOB, nausea, weakness)
  - Factors influencing size & course:
    - Thrombus size & location (proximal vs. distal)
    - Duration of ischemia
    - Collateral circulation
    - Coronary artery anatomy variation
    - Ischemic preconditioning
    - Cardioprotective mechanisms (eg, βBs, statins)
    - Circulatory stress (eg, tachycardia, HoTN, anemia)

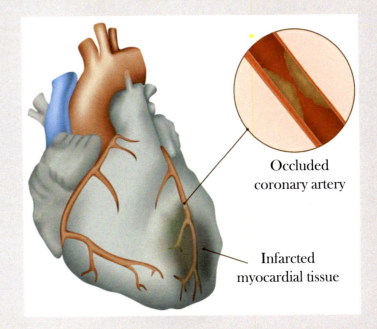

Occluded coronary artery

Infarcted myocardial tissue

Healthy coronary artery

Plaque formation

Thrombosis

85.0

ECG Classification of Ischemic Heart Disease

Key Points

➢ ECG classification of IHD: stable CAD vs. ACS

➢ Stable CAD = "stable angina"
- ✓ No ST-T changes at rest
- ✓ Ischemic ST-T changes w/ ↑O_2 demand
- ✓ QRS changes suggest prior MI

➢ ACS: STE vs. NSTE (affects management)
- ✓ STE-ACS: STE present
  - Nearly all develop MI = "STEMI"
- ✓ NSTE-ACS: STE absent
  - If MI develops = "NSTEMI"
  - If no MI develops = "unstable angina"

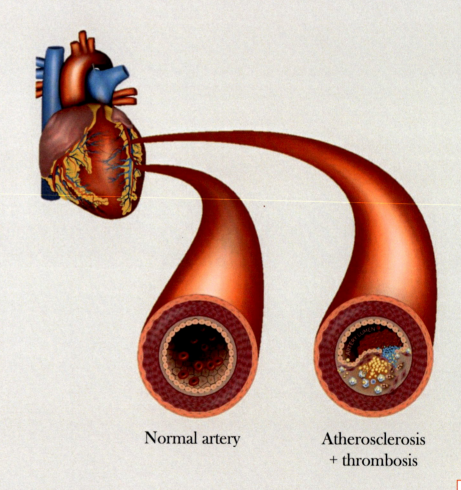

Normal artery   Atherosclerosis + thrombosis

ECG Basics in Myocardial Ischemia & Infarction

Key Points

ECG: cost-effective, valuable tool in dx, px, & tx of ischemia & infarction; allows for localizing, determining extent, & time course of ischemia

Myocardial ischemia: mainly affects repolarization → ST-T changes
- ✓ ST-segment deviation (elevation, depression): suggests acute ischemia
- ✓ Tw changes (inversion, flattened, hyperacute): often accompany ST-segment deviation in ischemia
  - Isolated Tw inversion/flattening: typically post-ischemic Tw changes & not signs of ischemia (except Wellen's syndrome)
  - Isolated hyperacute (broad & tall) Tw: ± ischemia
- ✓ ST-T changes: nonspecific, but strongly suggest ischemia if chest pain

Myocardial infarction: mainly affects depolarization → QRS changes
- ✓ Pathological Qw & Rw
- ✓ QRS fragmentation/notching
- ✓ ↓ Rw amplitude

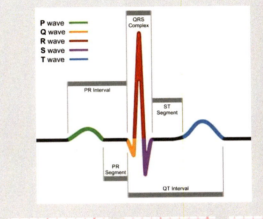

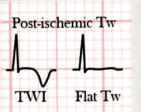
Post-ischemic Tw: TWI, Flat Tw

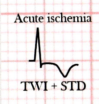
Acute ischemia: TWI + STD

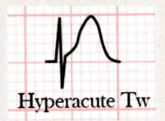
Hyperacute Tw

Convex STE | Straight upsloping STE | Straight horizontal STE | Straight downsloping STE

Downsloping STD

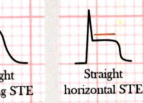
Horizontal STD

Pathological Qw

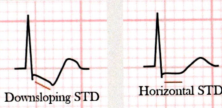

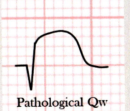

ST-T Basics in Acute Myocardial Ischemia

Key Points

- ST segment: from Jp to Tw onset; normally at baseline (PR segment); represents phase 2 (plateau) of AP
- ST-T transition: normally smooth; represents transition from phase 2 to 3 of AP; more abrupt transition in ischemia
- Tw: normally concordant w/ QRS in most leads; represents phase 3 (repolarization) of AP
  - I, II, -aVR, V5-V6: upright Tw
  - aVR: TWI
  - III: possible isolated TWI (normal if no TWI in aVF)
  - aVL: possible isolated TWI
  - aVF: often upright Tw, but sometimes flat Tw
  - V1: TWI (concordant w/ QRS) or flat Tw common (esp. females)
  - V7-V9: upright Tw
- ST-T changes: represent changes b/t Jp & end of Tw
  - Myocardial ischemia: affects phases 2 & 3 of AP
    - ST deviation: elevated or depressed Jp or J-60p from PR segment (use TP segment if PR segment difficult to discern)
    - Tw: flat, inverted, or ↑ amplitude
    - Depends on timing, localization, & extension of ischemia

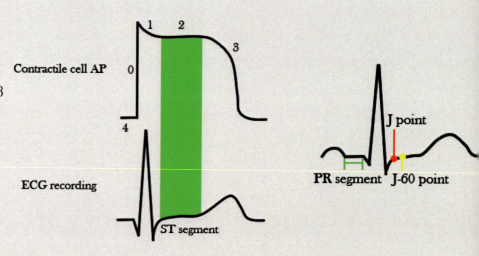
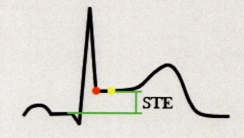
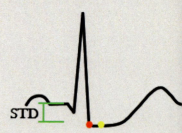

Injury Currents: Transmural vs. Subendocardial Ischemia

Key Points

- Myocardial ischemia: affects ventricular repolarization (phases 2 & 3) + resting potential (makes phase 4 less negative); also ↓ AP duration
  - ✓ AP differences → EP differences → electrical (injury) currents b/t normal & ischemic myocardium during systole (2/2 AP changes) & diastole (2/2 resting membrane potential changes) → ST-T changes
- Transmural ischemia: affects full wall (endocardium to epicardium)
  - ✓ ST vector: directed from endocardium to epicardium → STE in leads over ischemia + reciprocal STD in leads opposite ischemia
- Subendocardial ischemia: affects subendocardium
  - ✓ ST vector: directed from epicardium to endocardium → STD
  - ✓ Tw vector: ↓ AP duration may reverse repolarization → TWI
  - ✓ Note: STD + TWI not necessarily in leads over ischemic region; therefore, not reliable for localizing ischemia

You're doing great!

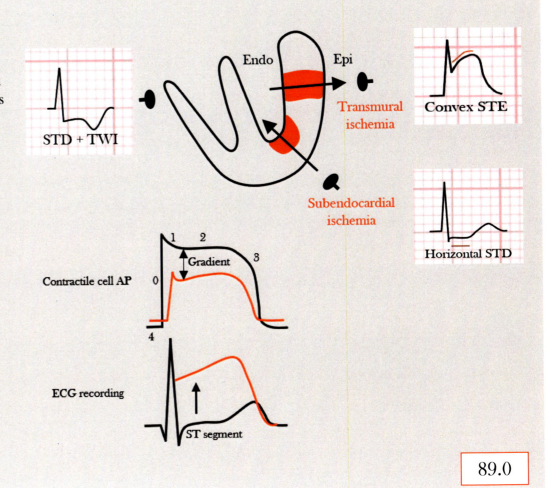

ECG Progression in Acute Myocardial Ischem[ia]

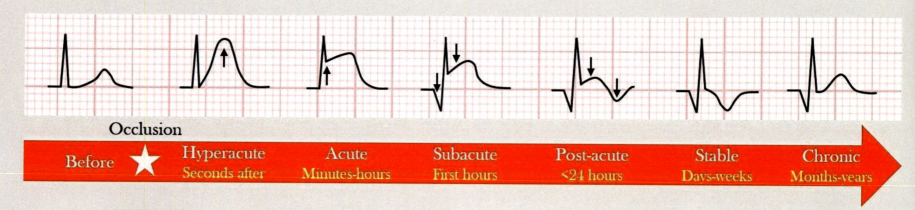

| Before | Occlusion ★ | Hyperacute
Seconds after | Acute
Minutes-hours | Subacute
First hours | Post-acute
<24 hours | Stable
Days-weeks | Chronic
Months-years |

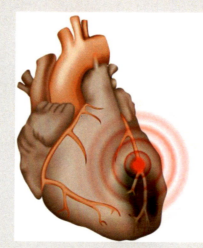

Elevation & Depression in Myocardial Ischemia

Key Points

Ischemic STD: horizontal (more specific) or downsloping
- ✓ ECG criteria: new horizontal or downsloping STD ≥0.5 mm in ≥2 anatomically contiguous leads (eg, II, III, & aVF; I & aVL)
- ✓ STEMI: represent 2° reciprocal changes (ie, mirror image of STE)
- ✓ NSTEMI or unstable angina: represent 1° changes; often associated w/ TWI or flat Tw
- ✓ Upsloping STD: rarely indicates ischemia (except tall Tw in most precordial leads = de Winter's sign; may suggest LAD occlusion); normal during exercise; normal if no TWI

Ischemic STE: convex, straight upsloping, straight horizontal, or straight downsloping; concave STE atypical of ischemia, but does not rule it out
- ✓ ECG criteria: based on age & sex; new STE in ≥2 anatomically contiguous leads
    - Males ≥40 y/o: ≥2 mm in V2-V3 or ≥1 mm in other leads
    - Males <40 y/o: ≥2.5 mm in V2-V3 or ≥1 mm in other leads
    - Females (any age): ≥1.5 mm in V2-V3 or ≥1 mm in other leads
    - V3R-V4R (male & female): ≥0.5 mm, but ≥1 mm in males <30 y/o
    - V7-V9 (male & female): ≥1 mm
- ✓ Jp close in height to Tw apex
- ✓ Often associated w/ reciprocal STD (suggests transmural ischemia; may be absent)

Common pitfalls: no STE on standard 12-lead ECG, but ischemia present
- ✓ Posterolateral ischemia: reciprocal STD in V1-V3; use posterior leads (STE in V7-V9)
- ✓ RV ischemia: use right-sided chest leads (STE in V4R-V5R)

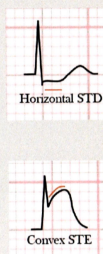
Horizontal STD

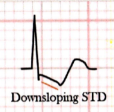
Downsloping STD

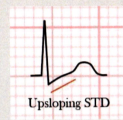
Upsloping STD

Convex STE

Straight upsloping STE

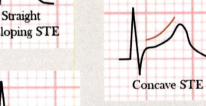
Concave STE

Straight horizontal STE

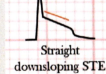
Straight downsloping STE

T-Wave Changes in Acute Myocardial Ischemia

Key Points

- Normal Tw: asymmetric w/ steeper downslope, concordant w/ QRS, smooth ST-T transition
  - Amplitude: ≤5 mm in limb leads & ≤10 mm in precordial leads; often greatest in V2-V3; proportional to QRS amplitude
  - Upright vs. inverted Tw: based on terminal Tw portion (also applies to biphasic Tw)
- Isolated TWI = TWI w/o ST-segment deviation
  - Does not indicate ischemia (except Wellen's syndrome)
  - Post-ischemic TWI: occurs *after* ischemia resolves; confirms ischemia occurred; ± negative Uw (↑ likelihood of ischemia); often resolve w/in days-weeks (may persist >1 year = chronic); normalization post-MI suggest some recovery of infarcted region
- Ischemic Tw: symmetric TWI, rarely >10 mm deep (reciprocal upright Tw changes in MI)
  - ECG criteria: ≥2 anatomically contiguous leads w/ [TWI ≥1 mm] + [Rw or Rw > Sw]
  - Hyperacute Tw: large, symmetric Tw w/ broad base (vs. narrow base in ↑ K); appear w/in seconds after total coronary artery occlusion; short-lived (except de Winter's sign)
- Non-ischemic TWI causes: RVH/LVH, RBBB/LBBB, preexcitation, PM-stimulated, etc.
  - Note: abnormal depolarization causes abnormal repolarization (ie, 2° ST-T changes)
  - Tw memory: TWI persists after depolarization normalizes (eg, TWI when not paced)
  - CVA (ICH): deep/gigantic, symmetric TWI in V1-V6 (± limb leads) ± ↑ QT interval
  - Hypertrophic CM: deep, isolated TWI in V2-V5 ± ↑ Rw & Sw amplitudes

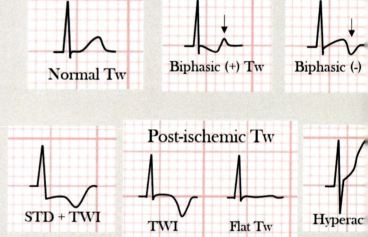

TWI: graded based on depth
- Flat Tw = 1 mm tall to 1 mm deep
- TWI = 1-5 mm deep
- Deep TWI = 5-10 mm deep
- Gigantic TWI = >10 mm deep

Wellen's Syndrome

Key Points
Wellen's syndrome: angina pectoris (last 24-48 hrs) + Wellen's sign
- ✓ Wellen's sign: following findings often in asymptomatic state
  - Deep, symmetric TWI in V1-V6 (at least V2-V5) ± I, aVL
    - Note: includes biphasic positive-negative Tw = TWI
  - No significant ST-segment deviation (± slight upsloping STE)
  - Normal to slightly ↑ troponins
- ✓ Clinical significance: severe, proximal LAD stenosis (acute or chronic); most develop massive anterior MI (↑ risk if TWI in I & aVL); ↑ risk of HF risk if no revascularization; immediate angiography required

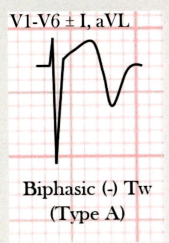

V1-V6 ± I, aVL

Biphasic (-) Tw (Type A)

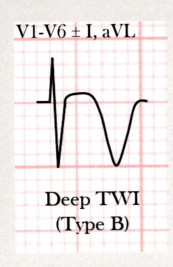

V1-V6 ± I, aVL

Deep TWI (Type B)

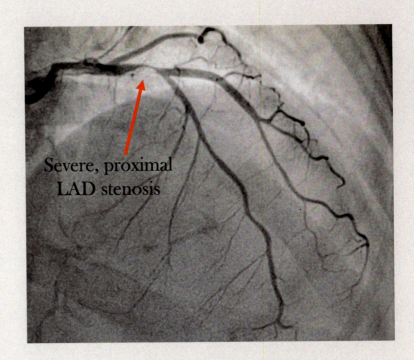

Severe, proximal LAD stenosis

de Winter's Sign

Key Points

- de Winter's sign: persistent hyperacute Tw syndrome
  - Large Tw: >5 mm in limb leads, >10 mm in precordial leads
  - Hyperacute Tw: large, symmetric Tw w/ broad base (vs. narrow base in ↑ K); appear w/in seconds after occlusion; often short-lived
  - ECG: upsloping STD (1-3 mm deep) + hyperacute Tw in V1-V6; often slight STE (>0.5 mm) in aVR
  - Clinical significance: acute proximal LAD occlusion; anterior STEMI equivalent w/o STE

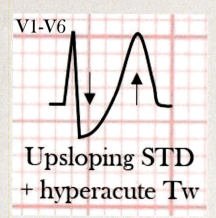

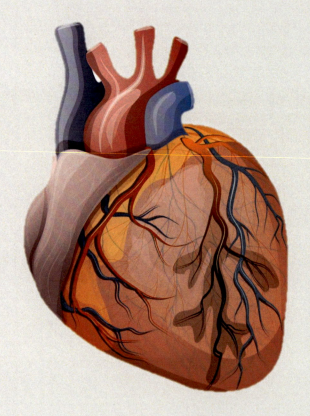

T-Wave Pseudonormalization

Key Points

Tw pseudonormalization: normalization of previously confirmed TWI during chest pain → suspect myocardial ischemia
- ✓ Applies regardless of initial TWI cause
    - LBBB w/ pseudonormalization in V5-V6, I, aVL → ischemia
    - Pseudonormalization of post-ischemic Tw → repeat ischemia

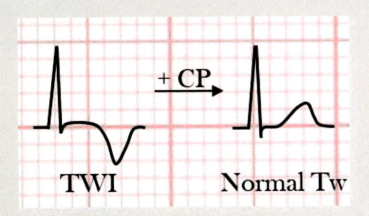

TWI +CP→ Normal Tw

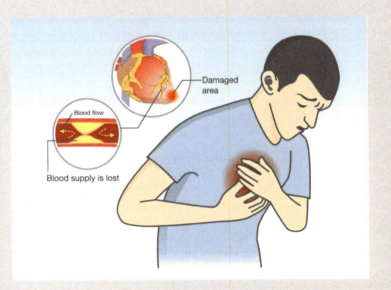

Pathological Q- & R-Waves

Key Points

➤ Pathological Qw: occur about 6-16 hours following symptom onset
  - ✓ Diagnose & localize prior MI (STE occurred in same leads)
  - ✓ Appear in transmural MI + extensive subendocardial MI
  - ✓ ↓ amplitude or resolve in about 1/3 patients post-inferior MI
  - ✓ ECG: ≥2 anatomically contiguous leads
    - V2-V3: [≥20 ms wide] or [QS complex]
    - Other leads: [≥30 ms wide + ≥1 mm deep] or [QS complex]
  - ✓ Normal variants:
    - aVL: small Qw if axis b/t +60° & +90°
    - V5-V6: small (septal) Qw
    - V1: isolated QS complex often acceptable (due to missing small Rw or misplaced electrode)
    - III: large isolated (respiratory) Qw (varies w/ respiration); small Qw if axis b/t -30° & 0° (not related to respiration)

➤ Pathological Rw: may diagnose prior MI
  - ✓ ECG: V1-V2 w/ [Rw ≥40 ms] + [R:S ≥1] + [concordant positive Tw] + [no conduction defect]

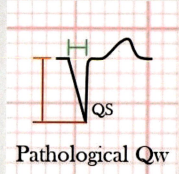

Pathological Qw

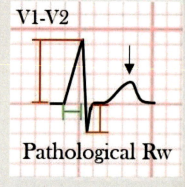

Pathological Rw

Coronary Artery Anatomy & Dominance

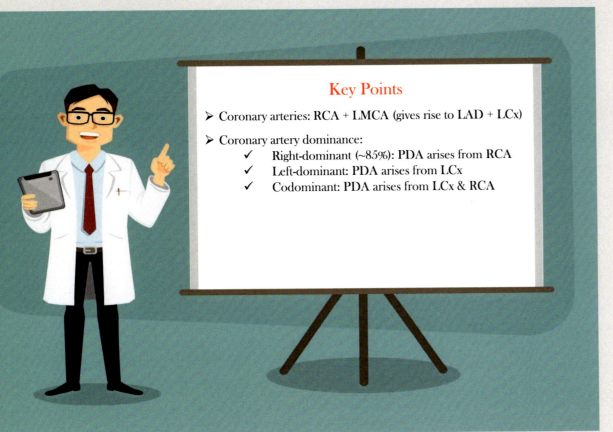

Key Points

- Coronary arteries: RCA + LMCA (gives rise to LAD + LCx)
- Coronary artery dominance:
    - ✓ Right-dominant (~85%): PDA arises from RCA
    - ✓ Left-dominant: PDA arises from LCx
    - ✓ Codominant: PDA arises from LCx & RCA

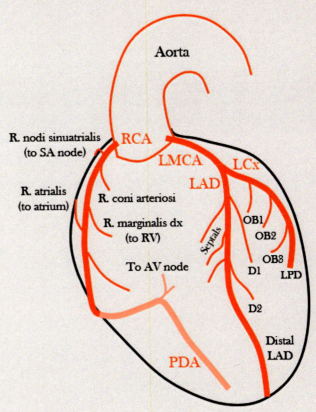

Left Ventricular Anatomy & Vascular Supply

Key Points
- LV: involved in any acute MI; bullet-shaped
  - Parts (long axis): basal, mid, & apical
  - Walls & vascular supply:
    - LAD supplies anterior & septal LV
    - RCA supplies inferior LV via PDA
    - LCx supplies lateral LV
  - Ischemia: subendocardium → epicardium

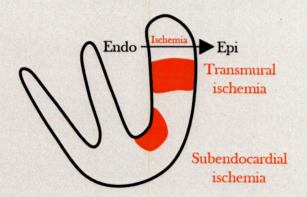
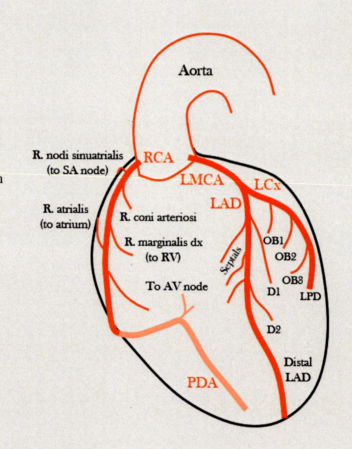
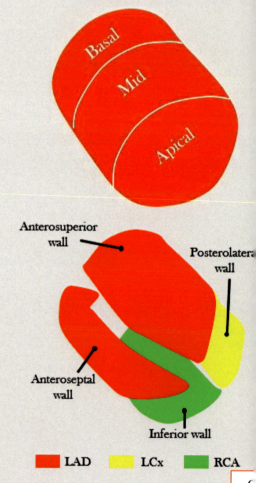

Localizing Ischemia in STEMI

Leads w/ STE	Ischemic Region	Occluded Artery
V1-V2	Septal	Proximal LAD
V3-V4	Anterior	LAD
V5-V6	Apical	Distal LAD, LCx, or RCA
I, aVL (reciprocal STD in II, III, aVF)	Lateral	LCx
III, aVF (reciprocal STD in I, aVL)	Inferior	RCA >>> LCx
V7-V9 (reciprocal STD in V1-V3)	Posterior (posterolateral or inferobasal)	RCA or LCx

I Lateral	aVR	V1 Septal	V4 Anterior
II Inferior	aVL Lateral	V2 Septal	V5 Lateral (apical)
III Inferior	aVF Inferior	V3 Anterior	V6 Lateral (apical)

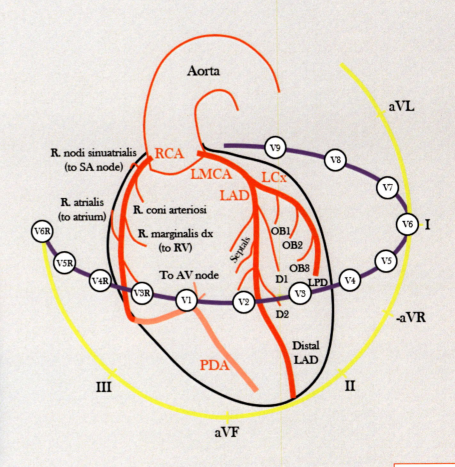

99.0

Right Coronary Artery Occlusion

Key Points

- RCA: supplies RV ± sinus node ± AV node ± posterior wall
  - If R-dominant: gives off PDA (supplies inferior LV + posterior 1/3 of IV septum)

- RCA occlusion: inferior MI ± RV MI (if proximal) ± posterior MI
  - Inferior MI: [STE in III > II, aVF] + [reciprocal STD in I & aVL]
  - Posterobasal (inferior + posterior) MI: [STE in II, III, aVF, V7-V9] + [reciprocal STD in I, aVL, V1-V3] ± [tall Rw & +Tw in V1-V3]
  - Inferior + RV MI: [STE in V3R-V6R ± V1 > V2]
    - ↓ STE duration in RV MI (thinner RV wall → faster infarct)

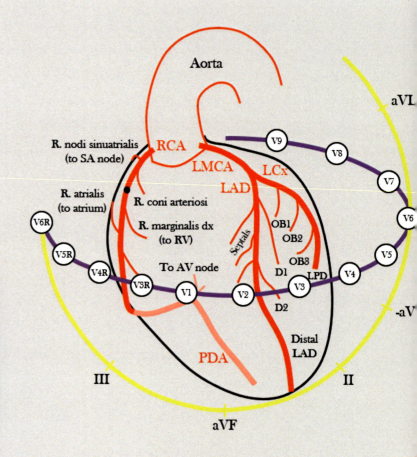

I Lateral	aVR	V1 Septal	V4 Anterior
II Inferior	aVL Lateral	V2 Septal	V5 Lateral (apical)
III Inferior	aVF Inferior	V3 Anterior	V6 Lateral (apical)

Left Anterior Descending Artery Occlusion

Key Points

LAD: supplies anterior 2/3 of IV septum (ie, anteroseptal area) + anterosuperior (anterior) wall + apical part of lateral wall ± inferoapical area ± inferior wall ("wrap-around LAD")

LAD occlusion: typically anterior MI [STE V1-V6, I, aVL] + [reciprocal STD in III, aVF ± II]
- ✓ Proximal LAD: affects basal parts of anterior wall, lateral wall ± IV septum
  - Proximal to 1st septal & 1st diagonal: [STE in V1-V6, I, aVL] + [reciprocal STD in II, III, aVF, aVR] ± RBBB
  - B/t 1st septal & 1st diagonal: often spares IV septum → as above w/o STE in V1
  - Distal to 1st septal & 1st diagonal: spares IV septum + basal parts of anterior wall → ST-vector directed inferiorly → only STE in V2-V6
- ✓ "Wrap-around LAD": inferior wall involved → [STE in II, III, aVF]; may resemble inferior MI from RCA occlusion
- ✓ 1st-diagonal branch: [STE in I & aVL] + [reciprocal STD in II, III, aVF]
- ✓ 1st septal perforator: [STE in V1-V2] + [reciprocal STD in V5-V6, II, III, aVF]
- ✓ "Septal" MI: STE in V1-V2 (appears to be more apical)

I	Lateral	aVR	aVR	V1	Septal	V4	Anterior
II	Inferior	aVL	Lateral	V2	Septal	V5	Lateral (apical)
III	Inferior	aVF	Inferior	V3	Anterior	V6	Lateral (apical)

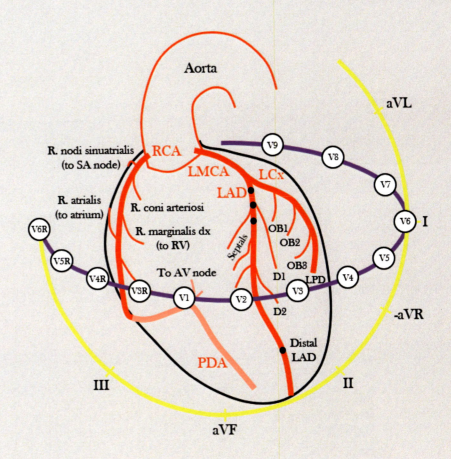

Left Circumflex Artery Occlusion

Key Points

- LCx: basal & mid parts of posterolateral LV ± inferior LV (if L-dominant via PDA) ± AV node
- LCx occlusion:
  - ✓ R-dominant: posterolateral (= posterior = inferobasal) MI → [STE in V7-V9] + [reciprocal STD in V1-V4] + [tall Rw & +Tw in V1-V4]
  - ✓ L-dominant: as above + inferior wall involved = inferoposterior MI → [STE in V7-V9, II, III, aVF ± I, aVL, but rarely V5-V6] + [reciprocal STD in V1-V4] + [tall Rw & +Tw in V1-V4]

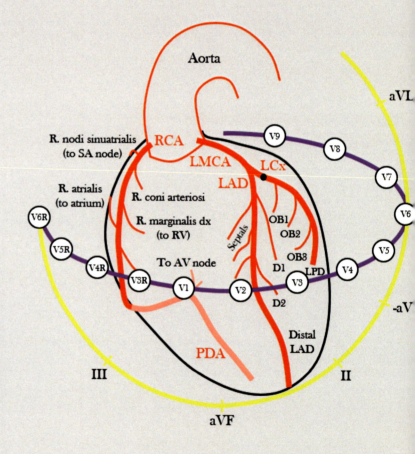

I Lateral	aVR	V1 Septal	V4 Anterior
II Inferior	aVL Lateral	V2 Septal	V5 Lateral (apical)
III Inferior	aVF Inferior	V3 Anterior	V6 Lateral (apical)

Left Main Coronary Artery Occlusion

Key Points

LMCA: gives rise to & supplies regions of LAD + LCx → massive MI
- ✓ L-dominant: gives off PDA (supplies inferior LV + posterior 1/3 IV septum)

LMCA occlusion (or LAD + LCx occlusion): affects anterosuperior, anteroseptal, & posterolateral walls ± inferior wall (if L-dominant); suspect if STE in most leads

ECG features: [STE in I, aVL, aVR, V1-V6] + [reciprocal STD in II, III, aVF]
- ✓ LMCA occlusion = [proximal LAD occlusion: STE in I, aVL, V1-V6] + [LCx occlusion: STD in V1-V4] → ↓ STE in V1-V4 (2/2 posterior STEMI)
- ✓ Basal septal/anterior MI → anterior-superior ST-vector → STE in aVR, aVL
    - STE in aVR: ≥ 1 mm & ≥ STE in V1; ↑ STE correlated w/ more severe disease & worse prognosis (independent of presentation)

Lateral	aVR	V1 Septal	V4 Anterior
Inferior	aVL Lateral	V2 Septal	V5 Lateral (apical)
Inferior	aVF Inferior	V3 Anterior	V6 Lateral (apical)

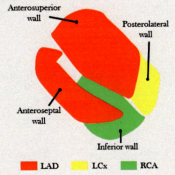

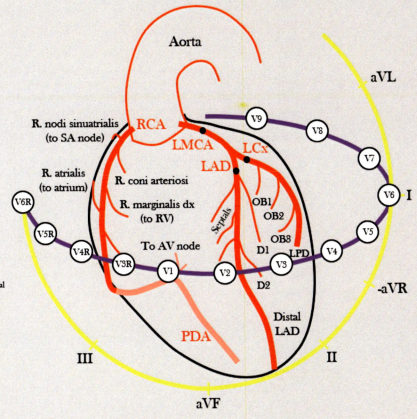

Prinzmetal's (Variant) Angina

Key Points

- Prinzmetal's (variant) angina: due to coronary artery vasospasm
  - Vasospasm & ischemia typically transient, resolving before MI
  - ECG: transient, localized STE (+ reciprocal STD) during chest pain followed by TWI (may persist for days to weeks)

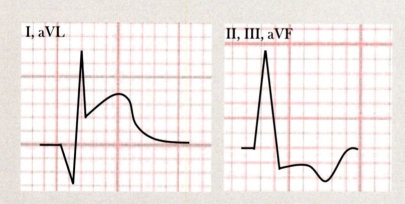

I, aVL   II, III, aVF

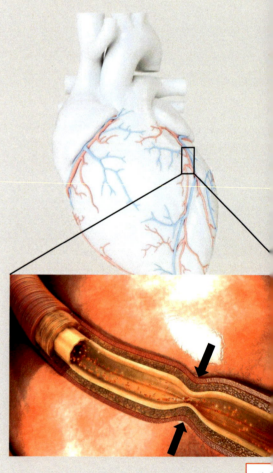

Conduction System Vascular Supply

Conduction System	Vascular Supply
Sinus node	RCA > LCx
AV node	RCA >>> LCx
His bundle	RCA ± septals of LAD
RBB	Septal branches of LAD ± RCA/LCx ± ventricular cavity
LBB	LAD ± RCA/LCx
LAF	LAD
LPF	Proximal: RCA ± septals of LAD Distal: septals of LAD

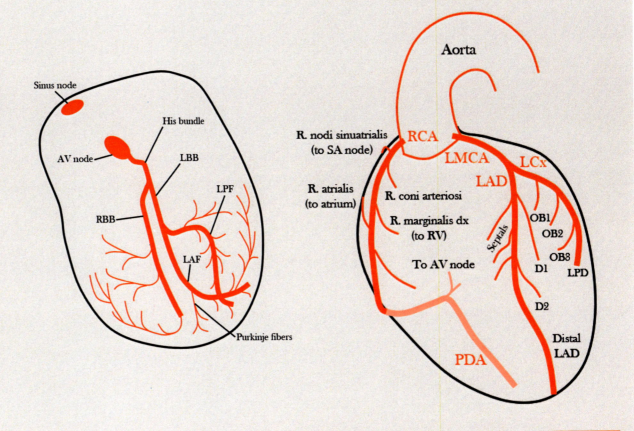

105.0

Conduction Defects in Myocardial Ischemia & Infarction

Key Points

- Conduction defects in ischemia & infarction:
  - Common: bradyarrhythmias, BBBs, fascicular blocks, AVBs
  - New-RBBB + chest discomfort → suggests acute ischemia (worse prognosis; often involves LAF)
    - Dx MI in LBBB can be difficult (Sgarbossa criteria)
    - RBBB affects terminal QRS & RV depolarization + weaker ST-T changes → apply infarct criteria (eg, pathological Qw)
  - Temporary autonomic dysfunction → AVBs + bradyarrhythmias
  - Inferior wall MI: often produces <u>transient</u> conduction defects
  - Anterior wall MI: often produces <u>permanent</u> conduction defects

Sgarbossa Criteria

Key Points

➤ LBBB: causes LV depolarization & repolarization changes → 2° QRS & ST-T changes → mimic or mask ischemia → use Sgarbossa criteria
  - ✓ Mimic ischemia: STE in V1-V2 + STD in I, aVL, V5-V6
  - ✓ Mask ischemia: due to stronger ST-T changes (vs. ischemia)

➤ Sgarbossa criteria: detects acute MI in LBBB or ventricular-paced rhythm
  - ✓ 2 points: discordant STE ≥5 mm in V1-V3
  - ✓ 3 points: STD ≥1 mm in V1-V3
  - ✓ 5 points: concordant STE ≥1 mm in V4-V6, I, aVL
  - ✓ ≥3 points: low sensitivity, but high specificity for acute MI

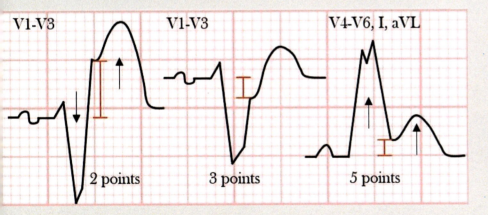

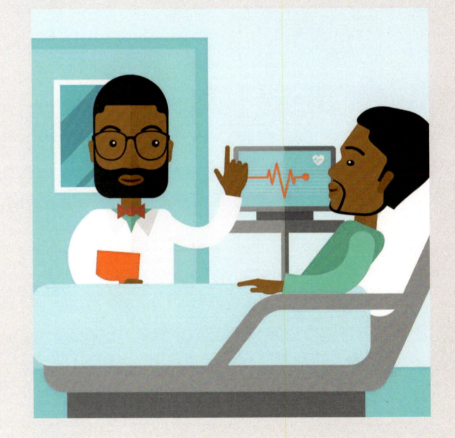

Conduction Defects in Inferior MI

Key Points
- Conduction defects 2/2 inferior wall MI: often transient, resolving spontaneously w/in 1 wk; sinus bradycardia > AVB
  - Sinus bradycardia & AVB 2/2 ↑ vagal tone: atropine-sensitive
  - AVB 2/2 edema or adenosine accumulation: often >24 hrs & resolves spontaneously; gradual normalization; atropine-insensitive
  - High-degree AVB: AVN defect (escape rhythm: <u>proximal</u> to His bifurcation → narrow QRS; <u>distal</u> to His bifurcation → wide QRS)

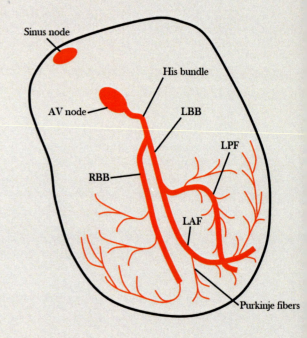

Conduction Defect	Comments	Prognosis
Sinus bradycardia	Most common	Due to ↑ vagal tone; often resolves w/in 1 wk
Sinus node dysfunction	Less common (may occur >24 hrs)	Often permanent
1st-degree AVB	Common	Often resolves w/in 1 wk
2nd-degree AVB Mobitz I	Relatively common	Often resolves w/in 1 wk
2nd-degree AVB Mobitz II	Uncommon (MC in anterior MI)	
3rd-degree AVB	Common (LC in anterior MI); gradually evolves 1st to 2nd to 3rd AVB → asymptomatic bradycardia	Due to intranodal defect; often resolves w/in 1 wk

Conduction Defects in Anterior MI

Key Points

- Conduction defects 2/2 anterior wall MI: often permanent (2/2 necrosis); caused by LAD artery occlusion → IV septum necrosis
    - AVB 2/2 His bundle necrosis → wide QRS escape rhythm
        - ↑ PR interval common
        - 2nd-degree AVB Mobitz II > I
        - 3rd-degree AVB: possible w/ extensive septal necrosis
    - RBBB: often precedes 3rd-degree AVB w/ LAD or RAD; QR complex in V1 (ie, pathological Qw); ± associated LAFB (↑ risk of 3rd-degree AVB esp. if 1st-degree AVB present → high mortality)

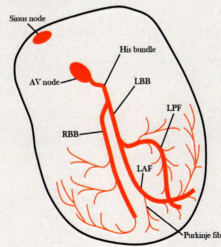
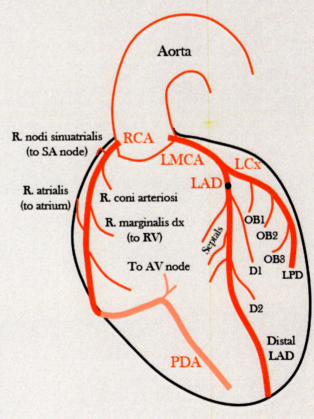

Part VI: Drugs & Electrolytes

TOPICS:

★ 110.0 Digoxin
111.0 Hypercalcemia
112.0 Hypocalcemia
★ 113.0 Hyperkalemia
114.0 Hypokalemia
115.0 Sodium & Magnesium Imbalances

★ High-Yield Topic

Digoxin

Key Points

Digoxin: ↑ contractility (inotropy) + ↓ HR (chronotropy)
- ✓ Inotropic effect: inhibits Na-K ATPase → ↑ [Na$^+$]i → ↑ [Ca^{2+}]i → ↑ Ca^{2+} binds actin & myosin → ↑ contractility
- ✓ Chronotropic effect: ↑ vagal activity → [↓ sinus node automaticity → ↓ HR] + [↓ AVN conduction]

ECG features:
- ✓ Generalized curved STD (most characteristic)
- ✓ Arrhythmias: at normal/toxic levels (unpredictable; ↓ K → ↑ effect)
  - Pro-arrhythmic 2/2 ↑ automaticity & ↓ AVN conduction
    - ↑ automaticity: PAC or PVC (early sign of overdose); atrial & ventricular tachyarrhythmias
    - ↓ AVN conduction: ↑ PR interval → AVB (often HR-dependent); SA block (typically transient)
- ✓ Toxicity: premature beats + AVB; bidirectional V-Tach

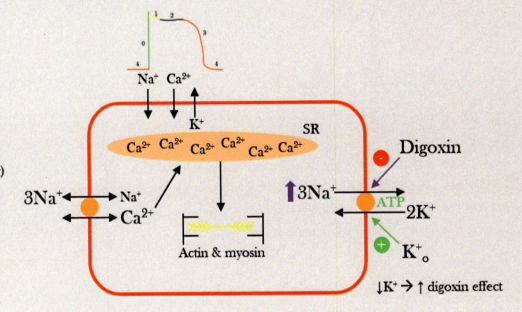

↓K$^+$ → ↑ digoxin effect

Bidirectional V-Tach

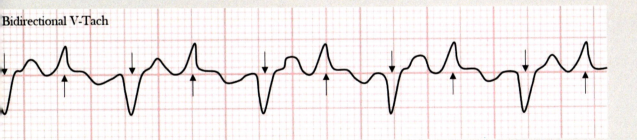

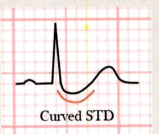

Curved STD

110.0

Hypercalcemia

Key Points

- Hypercalcemia: ↑ serum Ca^{2+}
  - Common causes: malignancies & 1° hyperparathyroidism
    - Others: sarcoidosis; thyrotoxicosis; familial hypocalciuric hypercalcemia; Addison's dz; renal failure; meds (lithium, tamoxifen, thiazides); immobilization; vit D/Ca^{2+} overdose
  - ECG features:
    - Most common: ↓ QT interval, ↑ QRS interval, bradycardia
    - ↑ QRS amplitude
    - ↓ Tw amplitude
    - Osborn waves (Jw)
    - AV block
    - STE in V1-V2
    - Sinus node dysfunction ± tachy-brady syndrome
    - Arrhythmias (V-Tach, V-Fib, TdP)

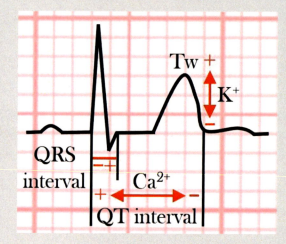

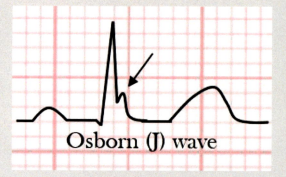

Osborn (J) wave

Hypocalcemia

Key Points

Hypocalcemia: ↓ serum Ca^{2+}
- ✓ Causes: acute pancreatitis; pancreatic/parathyroid surgery; alkalosis 2/2 hyperventilation; sepsis; rhabdomyolysis; abnormal Ca^{2+} absorption/resorption; renal failure; small bowel syndrome; ↑ calcitonin; meds (eg, phenytoin, bisphosphonates)
- ✓ ECG features:
    - Common: ↑ QT interval (TdP rare) & ↓ QRS interval
    - AV block
    - Sinus bradycardia
    - SA block
    - V-Fib

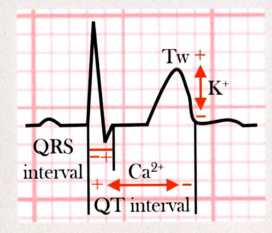

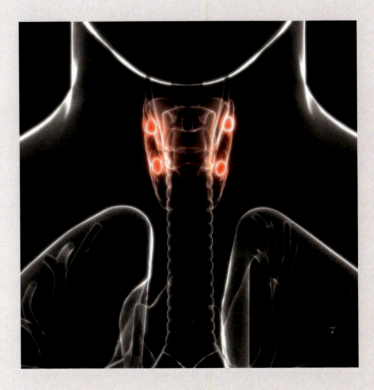

Hyperkalemia

Key Points

- Hyperkalemia: ↑ serum K^+ → slows impulse transmission
  - $[K^+]$: severity correlated w/ ECG changes & risk of arrhythmia
  - Causes: renal failure; acidosis; hemolysis; muscle damage; insulin deficiency; Addison's dz; meds (ACEi, ARB, K^+-sparing diuretics)
  - ECG features: based on severity
    - Mild hyper-K: pointed Tw (earliest sign; tall & narrow; prominent in precordial leads)
      - If LVH: normalization of 2° TWI in I, aVL, V5-V6
    - Moderate hyper-K: ↑ Pw duration, ↓ Pw amplitude, ↑ PR interval (± AVB), STE in V1-V3
      - If WPW syndrome: loss of delta wave
    - Severe hyper-K: ↑ QRS interval → sine wave → V-Fib

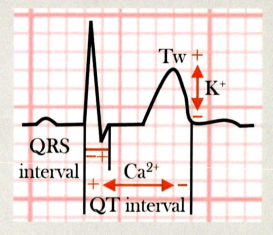

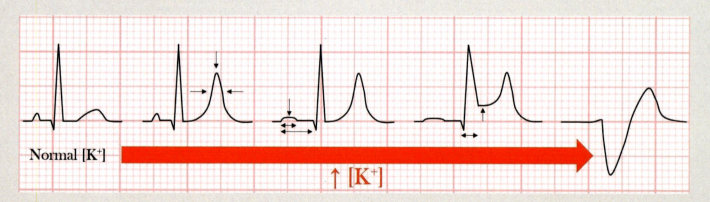

Hypokalemia

Key Points

➢ Hypokalemia: ↓ serum K^+ → myocardial hyperexcitability w/ potential to develop reentrant arrhythmias; check Mg^{2+} level
  - ✓ Causes: alcoholism; malnutrition; diarrhea; vomiting; 1° or 2° aldosteronism; glucose infusion; diuretics; corticosteroids; insulin
  - ✓ ECG features:
    - ↑ Tw duration + ↓ Tw amplitude (± TWI)
    - STD (note: if TWI present, can mimic ischemia)
    - ↑ Pw amplitude & duration ± ↑ PR interval
    - Uw: most prominent in precordial leads (esp. V2-V3)
      - If severe hypo-K: possible Uw > Tw amplitude
    - Apparent long QT interval (TU fusion → ↑ QU interval)
    - ± arrhythmias: monomorphic or polymorphic V-Tach (eg, TdP 2/2 acquired long QT syndrome)

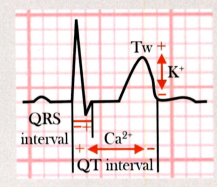

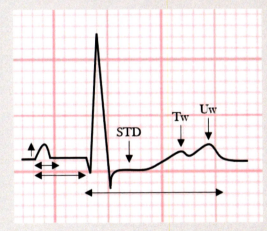

Sodium & Magnesium Imbalances

Key Points

- Hyper-/hypo-natremia: no effect on EKG, rhythm, or conduction

- Hypermagnesemia: rare; if severe, AV/IV conduction disturbances → complete heart block or asystole

- Hypomagnesemia: potentiate pro-arrhythmic effect of digoxin; predispose to SVT & ventricular tachyarrhythmias

Part VII: Artifacts

TOPICS:

116.0 Einthoven's Triangle
117.0 Left Arm-Right Arm Lead Reversal
118.0 Left Arm-Left Leg Lead Reversal
119.0 Right Arm-Left Leg Lead Reversal
120.0 Left Arm-Right Leg Lead Reversal
121.0 Right Arm-Right Leg Lead Reversal
122.0 Left Leg-Right Leg Lead Reversal
123.0 Bilateral Arm-Leg Lead Reversal
124.0 Precordial (Chest) Lead Reversal
125.0 Identifying the Culprit Electrode of Artifact
126.0 Motion Artifact
127.0 Muscle Artifact

EKG.MD

High-Yield Topic

Einthoven's Triangle

Key Points

- Einthoven's triangle: describes relationship b/t limb leads & electrodes
- Electrodes: LA, RA, LL, RL/N
- Leads: each reflects specific vector (magnitude + direction) produced by voltage differences from recording electrodes
  - Bipolar leads: I, II, III
    - I = LA − RA (directed at 0°)
    - II = LL − RA (directed at +60°)
    - III = LL − LA (directed at +120°)
  - Augmented unipolar leads: aVL, aVF, aVR
    - aVL = LA − (RA + LL)/2 (directed at -30°)
    - aVF = LL − (LA + RA)/2 (directed at +90°)
    - aVR = RA − (LA + LL)/2 (directed at -150°)
  - Wilson's central terminus (WCT): directionless "zero" lead
    - Limb lead signal average (WCT) = 1/3 (RA + LA + LL)

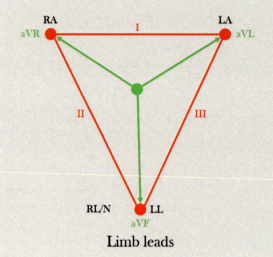

Limb leads

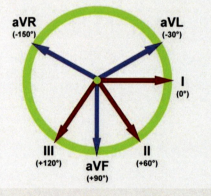

Left Arm-Right Arm Lead Reversal

Key Points

- LA-RA reversal: 180° horizontal rotation around aVF axis
  - Unchanged: aVF
  - Inverted: I
  - Switch places: II ↔ III; aVL ↔ aVR
  - Other clues: aVR often positive; marked RAD
  - May mimic dextrocardia (except normal Rw progression in precordial leads w/ LA-RA reversal)

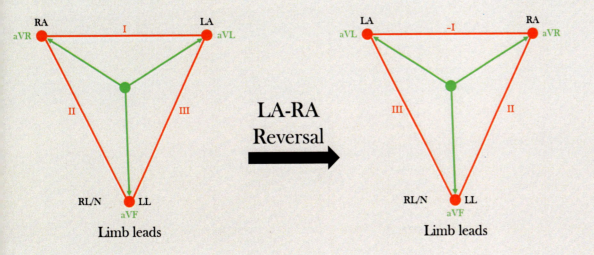

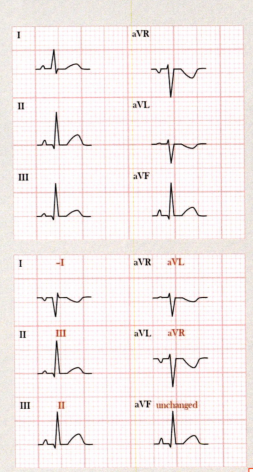

Left Arm-Left Leg Lead Reversal

Key Points
- LA-LL reversal: 180° vertical rotation around aVR axis
  - ✓ Unchanged: aVR
  - ✓ Inverted: III
  - ✓ Switch places: I ↔ II; aVL ↔ aVF
  - ✓ Other clues: larger Pw in I than II

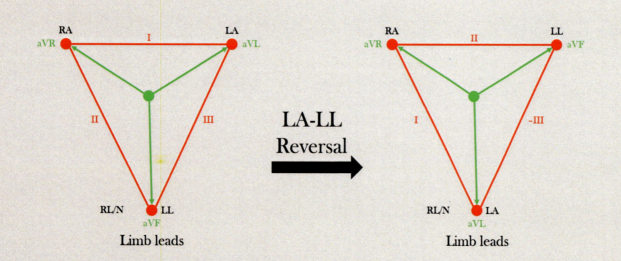

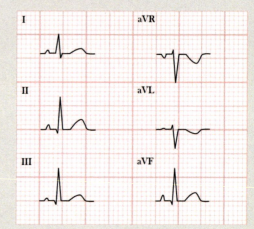

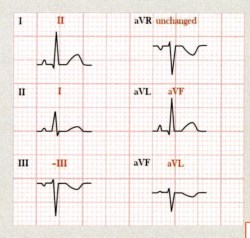

Right Arm-Left Leg Lead Reversal

Key Points

> RA-LL reversal: 180° vertical rotation around aVL axis
> - Unchanged: aVL
> - Inverted: II
> - Switch places: aVR ↔ aVF
> - Inverted + switch places: I ↔ III
> - Other clues: I, II, III, & aVF inverted; upright aVR

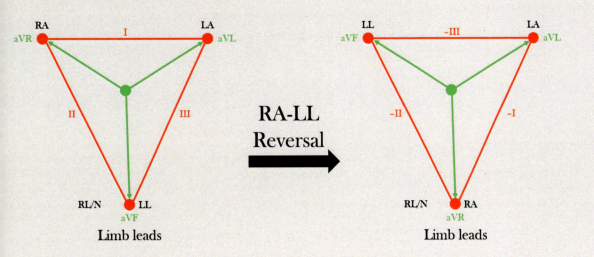
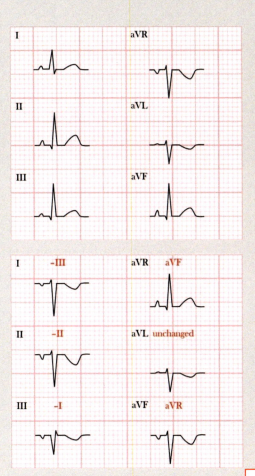

Left Arm-Right Leg Lead Reversal

Key Points

➢ LA-RL reversal: Einthoven's triangle collapses w/ RA at apex
- ✓ Unchanged: II
- ✓ aVR: inverted II
- ✓ Flat line (0 potential): III
- ✓ Identical: I & II; aVL & aVF
- ✓ Moving RL/N may distort precordial voltages

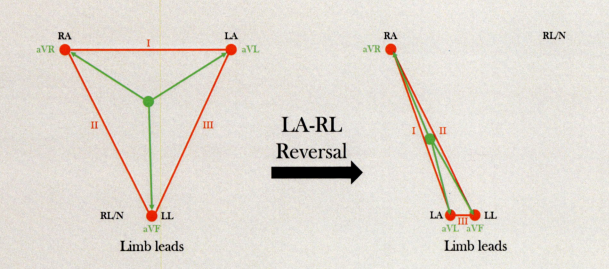

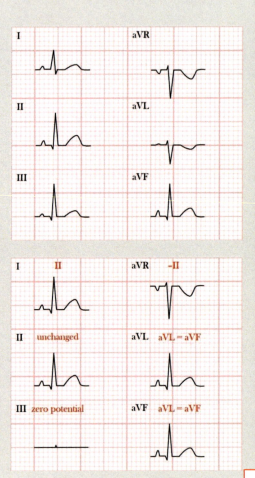

Right Arm-Right Leg Lead Reversal

Key Points

- RA-RL reversal: Einthoven's triangle collapses w/ LA at apex
  - Unchanged: III
  - I & aVL: inverted III
  - Flat line (0 potential): II
  - Identical: I & aVL; aVR & aVF
  - Moving RL/N may distort precordial voltages

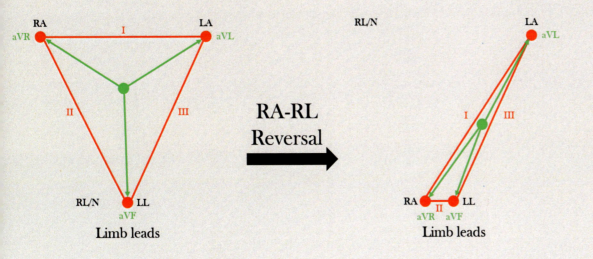

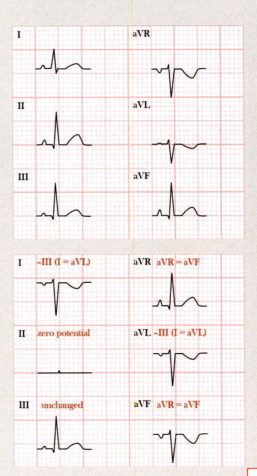

121.0

Left Leg-Right Leg Lead Reversal

Key Points
- LL-RL reversal: Einthoven's triangle preserved
  - Unchanged: all limb leads
  - Does not affect ECG interpretation

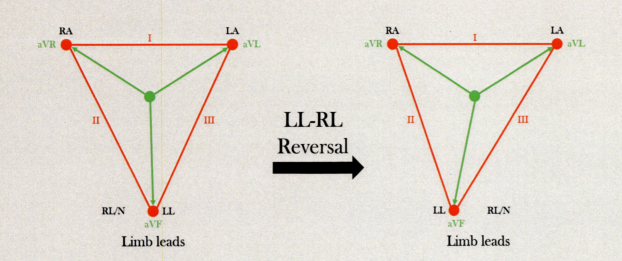
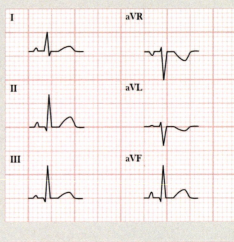
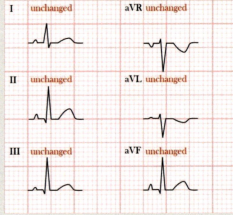

Bilateral Arm-Leg Lead Reversal

Key Points
➤ Bilateral arm-leg reversal: [LA-LL reversal] + [RA-RL reversal]; Einthoven's triangle collapses w/ LL at apex
- ✓ Inverted: III
- ✓ II & aVF: inverted III
- ✓ Flat line (0 potential): I
- ✓ Identical: II, III, & aVF; aVR & aVL (but different from baseline ECG)
- ✓ Moving RL/N may distort precordial voltages

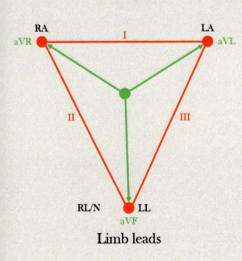
Limb leads

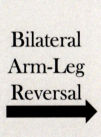

Bilateral Arm-Leg Reversal →

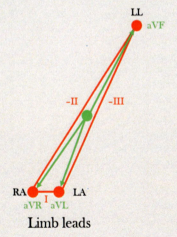
Limb leads

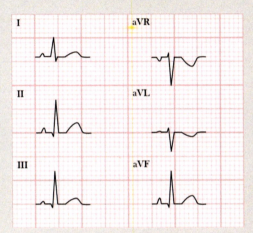

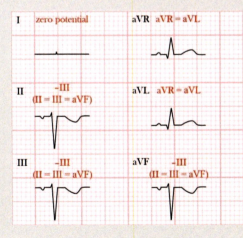

Precordial (Chest) Lead Reversal

Key Points

- Precordial (chest) lead reversal:
  - Normal Rw progression: ↑ Rw amplitude from V1-V5
  - Abnormal Rw progression: may suggest cardiac pathology or chest lead reversal (eg, abnormal Rw progression in V2-V4 may be due to V3-V4 reversal)

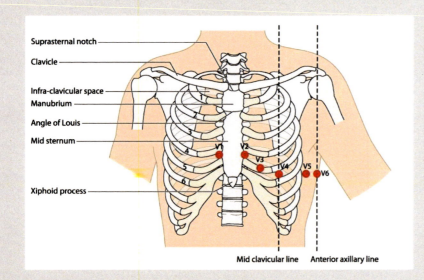

Normal Rw Progression

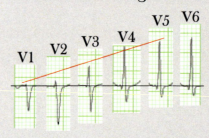

V3-V4 Reversal

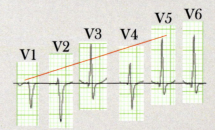

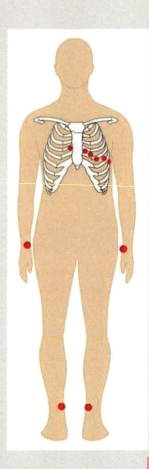

Identifying the Culprit Electrode of Artifact

Key Points

➢ Artifact: "artificial" & not from the heart (eg, motion, muscle, electrostatic, poor contact, electromagnetic interference, implanted stimulators)
  ✓ If in I & II, but not III → RA electrode
  ✓ If in I & III, but not II → LA electrode
  ✓ If in II & III, but not I → LL electrode
  ✓ If unique to 1 precordial lead → same precordial electrode

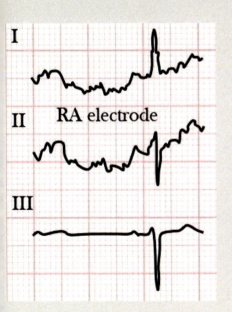

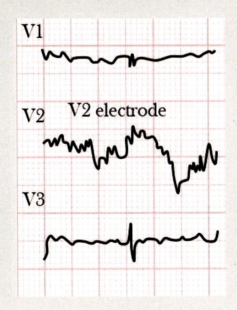

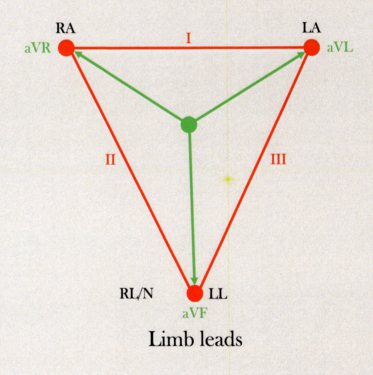

Limb leads

125.0

Motion Artifact

Key Points

- Motion artifact: skin stretches → voltage change in stratum lucidum
  - Respiration: low frequency (0.4-2 Hz)
    - To minimize: use gel; mildly abrade skin; take deep breath, let ½ out & hold while recording ECG
  - Movement: low frequency (1-3 Hz)
    - To minimize: use gel; mildly abrade skin; lie still & stop talking while recording ECG
  - Transport: medium frequency (3-15 Hz)
    - To minimize: use gel; mildly abrade skin; stop ambulance & record ECG

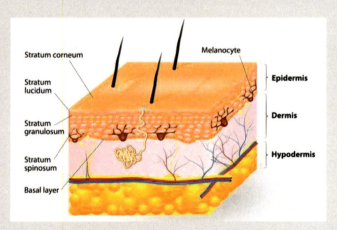

Respiration: low frequency (0.4-2 Hz)

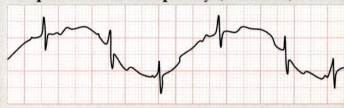

Movement: low frequency (1-3 Hz)

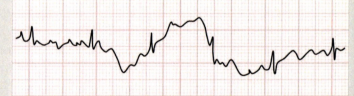

Transport: medium frequency (3-15 Hz)

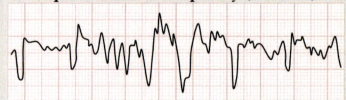

Muscle Artifact

Key Points
Muscle artifact: generated by skeletal muscle
- ✓ Muscle tension: high frequency (20-150 Hz)
  - To minimize: assure limbs supported & lying flat; ask patient to relax; consider meds if 2/2 pain; ↓ upper cutoff frequency filter (eg, 150 Hz to 40 Hz)
- ✓ Muscle tremor: high (20-150 Hz) &/or medium (3-5 Hz) frequency
  - To minimize: cover w/ blanket if 2/2 shivering; move limb electrode off culprit muscle; mildly abrade skin & check for dried skin if motion artifact

Muscle tremor: high frequency (20-150 Hz)

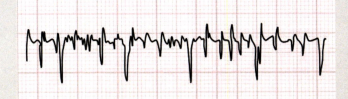

Muscle tension: high frequency (20-150 Hz)

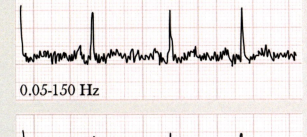

0.05-150 Hz

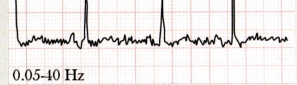

0.05-40 Hz

Part VIII: Inherited Arrhythmia Disorders

TOPICS:
★ 128.0 Brugada Syndrome
129.0 Long QT Syndrome
130.0 Short QT Syndrome
131.0 Arrhythmogenic Right Ventricular Dysplasia
132.0 J Wave Syndrome

★ High-Yield Topic

Brugada Syndrome

Key Points

- Brugada syndrome = Brugada pattern + SCD
  - Inherited arrhythmia disorder: [↑ risk of SCD] + [functional mutation(s)] + [absent overt structural HD] + [ECG pattern]
  - AD Na-channelopathy (SCN5A mutation); MC in males
  - Brugada pattern: pseudo-RBBB & persistent STE in V1-V3
    - Dynamic; may appear w/ rest, sleep, ↑ vagal tone, fever, Na-channel blockers, or vagotonic agents
    - 3 different patterns: type 1 most common

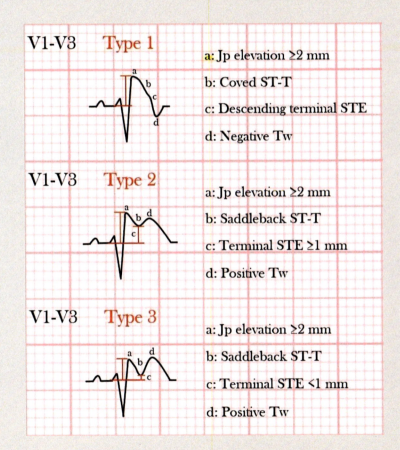

Brugada Patterns			
	Type 1	Type 2	Type 3
amplitude	≥2 mm	≥2 mm	≥2 mm
-T configuration	Coved	Saddleback	Coved &/or saddleback
minal ST segment	Gradually descending	Elevated ≥1 mm	Elevated <1 mm
	Negative	Positive or biphasic	Positive

Long QT Syndrome

Key Points

➢ **LQTS**: abnormally <u>slow</u> repolarization → prolonged QT → ↑ risk of fatal arrhythmias (eg, TdP)
  - ✓ Inherited arrhythmia disorder: [↑ risk of SCD] + [functional mutation(s)] + [absent overt structural HD] + [ECG pattern]
  - ✓ Inherited: ion-associated gene mutation (KCNQ1 → LQTS-1; KCNH2 → LQTS-2; SCN5A → LQTS-3)
  - ✓ Acquired: meds, electrolyte disturbance, myocardial ischemia
  - ✓ ECG features:
    - Prolonged QTc interval (≥440/460 ms M/F)
    - Tw morphology: depends on type LQTS
      - LQTS-1: early-onset, broad-based Tw
      - LQTS-2: low amplitude & notched Tw
      - LQTS-3: long, isoelectric ST w/ late, pointed Tw

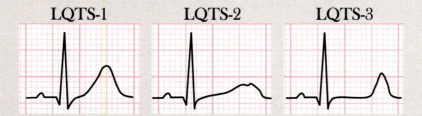

LQTS-1   LQTS-2   LQTS-3

LQTS Diagnostic Criteria: Schwartz Score	Points
ECG Findings	
QTc (using Bazett formula: $QTc = \frac{QT}{\sqrt{RR}}$)	
≥480 ms	3
460-470 ms	2
450 ms & male gender	1
QTc at 4th minute of recovery from exercise stress ≥480 ms	1
TdP	2
Tw alternans	1
Notched Tw in 3 leads	1
Low HR for age (children), resting HR <2% for age	0.5
Clinical History	
Syncope (cannot receive points for syncope & TdP)	
With stress	2
Without stress	1
Congenital deafness	0.5
Family History	
Other family members with definite LQTS	1
Sudden death in immediate family members (before 30 y/o)	0.5

SCORE: ≤1 point = low probability; 1.5-3 points = intermediate probability; ≥3.5 points = high probability

Short QT Syndrome

Key Points

Short QT syndrome: abnormally <u>rapid</u> repolarization (→ short QT) at various rates → ↑ risk of fatal arrhythmias

- ✓ Inherited arrhythmia disorder: [↑ risk of SCD] + [functional mutation(s)] + [absent overt structural HD] + [ECG pattern]
- ✓ Mechanism: (1) short atrial/ventricular refractory periods + (2) transmural dispersion of repolarization → ↑ risk of arrhythmia
- ✓ Inherited: ion-associated gene mutation (KCNH2 (IKr)→ SQTS-1; KCNQ1 (IKs) → SQTS-2; KCNJ2 (IK1) → SQTS-3; CACNA1C (ICaL)→ SQTS-4; CACNB2B (ICaL) → SQTS-5)
- ✓ Acquired: ↑ T, ↑ H$^+$, ↑ K$^+$, ↑ Ca^{2+}, autonomic tone changes
- ✓ ECG features:
    - Short QTc interval (<330/340 ms M/F)
        - All w/ QT <320 ms & QTc <340 ms
    - Lack normal QT interval changes w/ HR
    - Peaked & narrow Tw (esp. precordial leads)
    - Short or absent ST segments
    - Episodic A-Fib or V-Fib

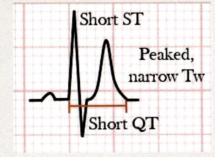

SQTS Diagnostic Criteria	Points
ECG Findings	
QTc (using Bazett formula: QTc = $\frac{QT}{\sqrt{RR}}$)	
<370 ms	1
<350 ms	2
<330 ms	3
J point-T peak interval <120 ms (measured in precordial lead w/ greatest Tw amplitude)	1
Clinical History (w/o identifiable cause)	
H/o sudden cardiac arrest	2
Documented polymorphic V-Tach or V-Fib	2
Unexplained syncope	1
A-Fib	1
Family History	
1st- or 2nd-degree relative w/ high probability of SQTS	2
1st- or 2nd-degree relative w/ autopsy-negative SCD	1
Sudden infant death syndrome (SIDS)	1
Genotype	
Genotype positive	2
Mutation of undetermined significance in a culprit gene	1
SCORE: ≤2 points = low probability; 3 points = intermediate probability; ≥4 points = high probability	

Arrhythmogenic Right Ventricular Dysplasia

Key Points

- ARVD: fibrofatty RV myocardium replacement → paroxysmal ventricular arrhythmias & risk of SCD
  - Inherited arrhythmia disorder: [↑ risk of SCD] + [functional mutation(s)] + [absent overt structural HD] + [ECG pattern]
    - Typically AD w/ variable penetrance & expression; AR form exists (Naxos disease: woolly hair & palmoplantar keratoderma)
    - More common in males + Italian/Greek descent
  - No single diagnostic test; consider clinical, ECG, & imaging findings
  - Clinical findings: palpitations, syncope, & cardiac arrest 2/2 exercise; SCD; FHx of SCD; RV failure → biventricular failure & dilated CM
  - ECG features:
    - Epsilon wave (most specific)
    - V1-V3: [TWI] + [Sw upstroke ≥55 ms] + [QRS interval ≥110 ms]
    - Paroxysmal episodes of reentrant RV V-Tach (LBBB morph)
  - Imaging:
    - ECHO: dilated, hypokinetic RV w/ prominent apical trabeculae & RVOT dilatation
    - Cardiac MRI: fibrofatty infiltration; RV thinning, dilatation, &/or aneurysm; wall motion abnormalities; global systolic dysfunction
    - CT scan; RV contrast angiography; histology via biopsy (definitive)
  - High risk if: h/o syncope 2/2 cardiac arrest, recurrent arrhythmias not suppressed by antiarrhythmic, or FHx cardiac arrest in 1st-degree relative

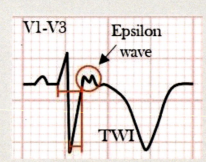
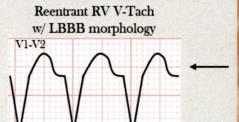
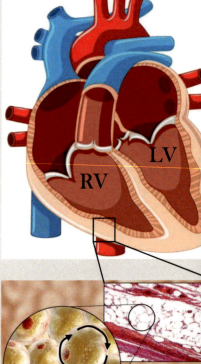

Part IX: Miscellaneous

TOPICS:

32.0 Hypothermia

33.0 Intracranial Hemorrhage

34.0 Early Repolarization

35.0 Acute Pericarditis

36.0 Pericardial Effusion & Cardiac Tamponade

High-Yield Topic

EKG.MD

Hypothermia

Key Points

- Hypothermia (<35°C): mild 32-35°C; moderate 29-32°C; severe <29°C
  - ECG features:
    - Bradyarrhythmias (eg, sinus bradycardia, A-Fib w/ slow ventricular response, slow junctional rhythms, AVB)
    - Widening of PR interval, QRS interval, & QT interval
    - Muscle tremor artifact 2/2 shivering
    - Osborn wave (Jw): positive deflection at Jp (negative in aVR & V1; prominent in precordial leads; amplitude proportional to degree of hypothermia; ± STD & TWI)
    - Ventricular ectopic beats & arrhythmias (V-Tach, V-Fib)

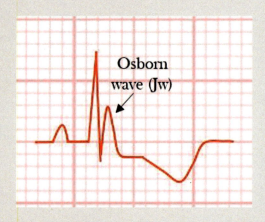

Intracranial Hemorrhage

Key Points
- ICH: bleeding into intracerebral/subarachnoid spaces
  - Trauma/HTN → ICH → ↑ ICP → Cushing reflex:
    1. Irregular or ↓ respirations (2/2 impaired brainstem)
    2. Bradycardia
    3. Systolic HTN (widens pulse pressure)
  - ECG features:
    - "Cerebral Tw": deep (≥5 mm), wide, symmetric TWI in V1-V6 ± limb leads (cerebrovascular insult pattern)
    - Prolonged QTc interval
    - Bradyarrhythmias
    - ± STD or STE ("neurogenic stunned myocardium"), ↑ Uw amplitude, arrhythmias (sinus tachycardia, junctional rhythms, PVCs, A-Fib)

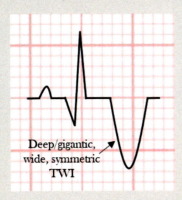

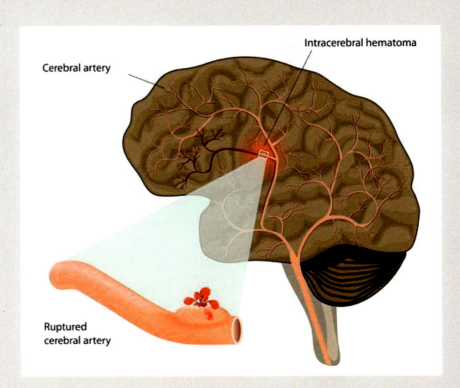

Early Repolarization

Key Points

➢ Early repolarization: considered "benign", but ↑ risk SCD (esp. in II, III, aVF)
  ✓ End-QRS notch/slur descriptors: $J_{onset} - J_{peak} - J_{termination}$
    ▪ If chest pain: measure STE at $J_{termination}$
  ✓ ECG criteria:
    1. End-QRS notch &/or slur on downslope of prominent Rw
       ✓ End-QRS notch: must be entirely above baseline
       ✓ End-QRS slur: must start before baseline reached
    2. J_{peak} ≥1 mm in ≥2 anatomically contiguous leads (excluding V1-V3)
    3. QRS duration <0.12 s (120 ms)
    *Other features: concave STE (esp. precordial leads); ↑ Tw amplitude

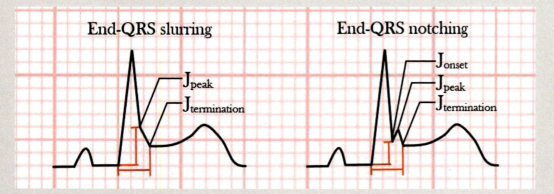

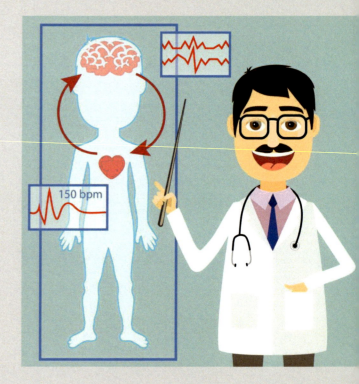

Acute Pericarditis

Key Points

- Acute pericarditis: inflammation of pericardium
  - Causes: infection (esp. viral); RA; SLE; acute MI; post-MI (Dressler syndrome); radiation exposure; trauma; uremia; TB; neoplasms; post-cardiac surgery (hemorrhagic pericarditis)
  - Clinical findings: positional chest pain (inspiration & supine position worsens; sitting upright & leaning forward alleviates); ↑ HR; cold sweats; anxiety; pericardial friction rub; ↑ troponins; pericardial effusion (ECHO) → cardiac tamponade
  - ECG features: static & slow changes over days to weeks
    - Generalized concave STE (<4 mm, ± Jp notch) & PRD
    - Reciprocal STD & PRE in aVR ± V1
    - General course: STE → STE resolves + Tw flattening → TWI → normal ECG
    - Sinus tachycardia (common)

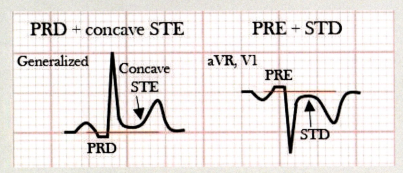

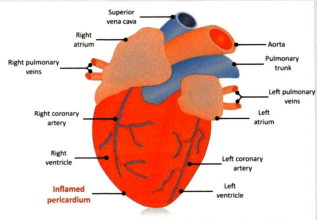

135.0

Pericardial Effusion & Cardiac Tamponade

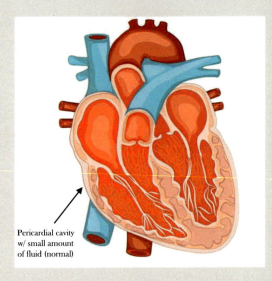

Pericardial cavity w/ small amount of fluid (normal)

Key Points

- Pericardial effusion: abnormal ↑ fluid in pericardial cavity; if continued accumulation → ↑ intra-pericardial pressure → disturbs ventricular filling & relaxation → hemodynamic changes → cardiac tamponade (HoTN, muffled heart sounds, JVD)
  - Causes: pericarditis (#1); infections (eg, viral, bacterial, TB); postpericardiotomy syndrome; acute transmural MI; ventricular free wall rupture; neoplasms (esp. breast/lung cancer); aortic dissection rupture into pericardium; inflammatory conditions (eg, RA, SLE, scleroderma, rheumatic fever); idiopathic; renal failure; hypothyroidism; hypercholesterolemia; Dressler syndrome; irradiation; trauma; iatrogenic damage to pericardium
  - ECG features:
    - Low QRS voltage
    - Electrical alternans (hallmark of cardiac tamponade)
    - Sinus tachycardia
    - ± PQ segment depression

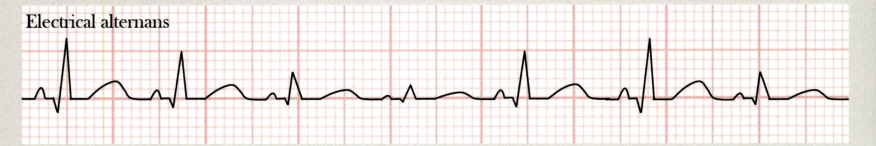

Electrical alternans

Part X: Congenital Heart Disease

TOPICS:
147.0 Congenital Heart Disease
148.0 Atrial Septal Defects
149.0 Ostium Secundum Atrial Septal Defect
150.0 Ostium Primum Atrial Septal Defect
151.0 Sinus Venosus Atrial Septal Defect
152.0 Atrioventricular Septal Defect (AV Canal)
153.0 Ventricular Septal Defect
154.0 Patent Ductus Arteriosus
155.0 Aortopulmonary Window
156.0 Pulmonary Valve Stenosis
157.0 Aortic Valve Stenosis
158.0 L-Transposition of the Great Vessels
149.0 Anomalous Left Coronary Artery from the Pulmonary Artery
150.0 Anomalous Origin of Left or Right Coronary Artery from the Contralateral Sinus of Valsalva
151.0 Left Ventricular Noncompaction
152.0 D-Transposition of the Great Arteries
153.0 Tetralogy of Fallot
154.0 Truncus Arteriosus
155.0 Pulmonary Atresia with Intact Ventricular Septum
156.0 Ebstein's Anomaly
157.0 Tricuspid Atresia
158.0 Hypoplastic Left Heart Syndrome
159.0 Single Ventricle Defects
160.0 Fontan Palliation

Congenital Heart Disease

Key Points

- ECG useful for: screening (+ PE) & monitoring disease severity & progression
  - Normal ECG + PE → reassure no structural HD
- ECG clues:
  - Atrial enlargement or ventricular hypertrophy → congenital heart disease
  - AV conduction abnormalities → ventricular inversion
  - Ventricular preexcitation → Ebstein's anomaly of tricuspid valve
  - Leftward QRS axis → ostium primum ASD, AV canal defect, tricuspid atresia

Acyanotic Lesions
- ASD
- AV canal defect
- VSD
- PDA
- Aortopulmonary window
- Pulmonic stenosis
- Aortic stenosis
- L-transposition of great vessels
- ALCAPA
- LV noncompaction

Cyanotic Lesions
- d-transposition of great vessels
- Tetralogy of Fallot
- Truncus arteriosus
- Pulmonary atresia w/ intact ventricular septum
- Ebstein's anomaly of tricuspid valve
- Tricuspid atresia
- Hypoplastic left heart syndrome
- Single ventricle

Atrial Septal Defects

Key Points

Pathophysiology:
- Acyanotic septal defect b/t atria; occurs during fetal heart development
- Major ASD types:
    1. Ostium secundum ASD (MC, 70%; septum primum defect)
    2. Ostium primum ASD (inferior septum defect; ± AV canal defects)
    3. Sinus venosus ASD (lumen defect; SVC > IVC)
- LA → LV (birth) or RA (↑ age) depends on relative ventricular compliance
- ASD → L-to-R shunt → R-sided volume overload → pHTN (pulmonary vascular obstructive disease) → RVH → RAE → R-to-L shunt reversal

Presentation: asymptomatic 3 y/o + new murmur
- 2/6 systolic ejection murmur at LUSB; wide fixed-split S2

ECG features: normal, axis deviation, RVH, RAE, atrial arrhythmias, RVCD
- Crochetage pattern (secundum): notching near R wave apex in II, III, aVF

Treatment: catheter or surgical correction
- Surgical complication: postpericardiotomy syndrome (1-6 wks post-op)

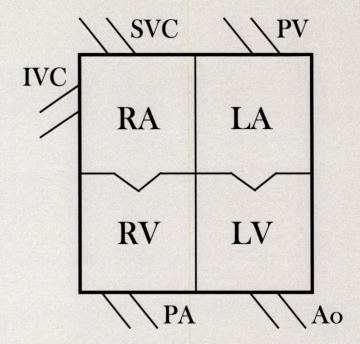

Ostium Secundum Atrial Septal Defect

Key Points

- Ostium secundum ASD: MC (70%); septum primum defect
- ECG features:
  - NSR; normal Pw amplitude & duration
    - ± peaked Pw in II (RAE); ± ↑ Pw duration/dispersion
  - Age-related: ↑ PR interval & ↑ HV interval
  - ↑ L-to-R shunt: RVCD + RVH with rsR' pattern in V1
  - RVH if ≥1:
    1. qR pattern or upright Tw in V1-V2
    2. ↑ Rw amplitude in V1
    3. Sw amplitude in V6 >95th percentile
    4. Abnormal R/S ratio in V1 (>1) or V6 (<1)
  - 87% sensitivity, 96% specific for dx: rsR' (V1) ± RVH or RVH w/o rsR' (V1)
  - Crochetage pattern: notching near R wave apex in II, III, aVF
    - 32% sensitivity; 1 lead = 86% specificity; 3 leads = 92% specificity
  - Arrhythmias if unrepaired: A-Flut; A-Fib; sinus brady w/ junctional escape
  - Surgical closure: ? ↓ P wave duration & dispersion (persistent A-Fib risk)
    - Arrhythmias: ↓ A-Flut; no change in A-Fib
  - Transcatheter closure: partial/complete regression of ECG abnormalities
    - ↓ QT interval dispersion w/in 1-mo (other intervals unchanged)
    - Postprocedural AVB (transient)
    - Arrhythmias: rare & benign (long-term data lacking)

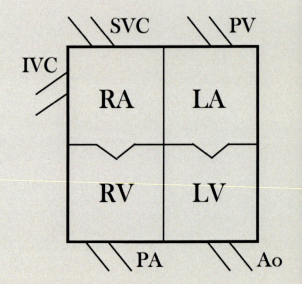

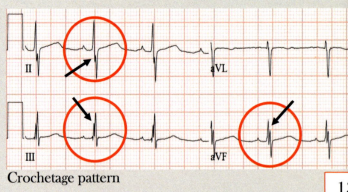

Crochetage pattern

Ostium Primum Atrial Septal Defect

Key Points
- Ostium primum ASD: anterior & inferior atrial septum defect
  - Associations: AV canal defects; cleft MV → MR; trisomy 21
- ECG features:
  - Often normal sinus & AV node function
  - Pw changes of RAE/LAE rare
  - ↑ PR interval common if associated AV canal defect
    - Due to prolonged intraatrial conduction
  - QRS axis (frontal plane): LAD (CCW QRS vector loop)
    - Due to (1) posterior & inferior AV node & LBB displacement; (2) relative LAF hypoplasia
  - If significant MR associated w/ cleft MV: RVCD + RVH ± LVH
  - Surgical repair risks: post-op AVB; postpericardiotomy syndrome

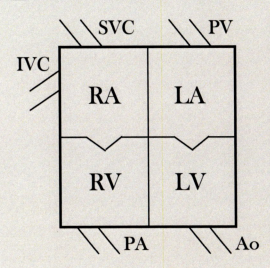

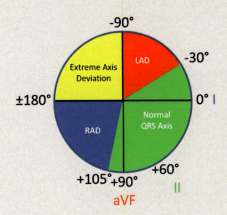

Sinus Venosus Atrial Septal Defect

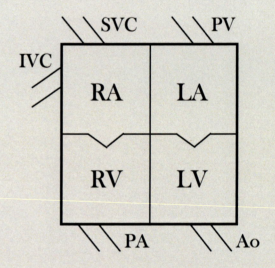

Key Points

- Sinus Venosus ASD: lumen defect; (1) SVC > (2) IVC
  - Associations: anomalous pulmonary venous drainage of PV into SVC, IVC, RA → L-to-R shunt
- ECG features:
  - Pw axis (frontal plane; sinus rhythm): leftward + superior or normal
  - Ectopic atrial rhythm: negative Pw in II, III, aVF (low atrial rhythm)
  - QRS axis (frontal plane): RAD
  - Post-surgical repair risks:
    - Sinus node dysfunction & age-related A-Fib
      - Alternative surgical approaches may ↓ frequency
    - Postpericardiotomy syndrome

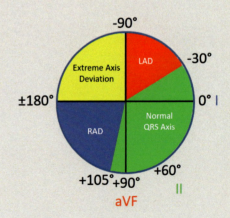

Atrioventricular Septal Defect (AV Canal)

Key Points

- AV septal defect (AV canal; endocardial cushion defect):
  - (1) ASD (ostium primum), (2) VSD, & (3) common AV valve
  - Associations: Down syndrome (trisomy 21)
  - Risks: pulmonary vascular obstructive disease; endocarditis
- ECG features:
  - Often normal sinus & AV node function
  - Pw changes of RAE/LAE rare
  - ↑ PR interval (2/2 prolonged intraatrial conduction)
  - QRS axis (frontal plane): LAD (CCW QRS vector loop)
    - Due to (1) posterior & inferior AV node & LBB displacement; (2) relative LAF hypoplasia
  - If significant MR associated w/ cleft MV: RVCD + RVH ± LVH
  - Surgical repair risks: post-op AVB; postpericardiotomy syndrome

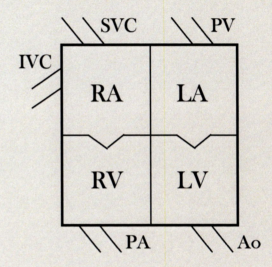

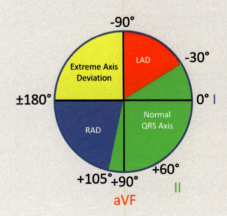

Ventricular Septal Defect

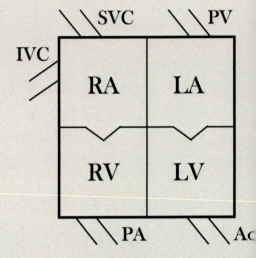

Key Points

- VSD: septal defect b/t ventricles; occurs during fetal heart development; #1 CHD
    - Causes: Down syndrome, fetal alcohol syndrome, idiopathic
    - Types:
        1. Muscular VSD (MC; lower, muscular portion)
        2. Perimembranous VSD (upper, membranous portion)
        3. AV canal type VSD (AV canal defect; below TV & MV)
        4. Conal septal VSD (rarest; below PV)
    - L-to-R shunt; holosystolic murmur at LLSB; defect size matters
- ECG features: reflect degree of hemodynamic abnormality
    - Small isolated VSD with minimal L-to-R shunt: normal ECG
    - Moderate-to-large VSD: RVH possible (esp. if ↑ RV pressure)
    - Large VSD with large L-to-R shunt: RVH + LAE + LVH
        - RVH: prominent R (V1) or S (V6); R:S >1 (V1) or <1 (V6)
        - LAE: prominent, wide terminal negative Pw in V1
        - LVH: deep, narrow Qw + prominent Rw in II, III, aVF & V5-V6
        - BVH: *Katz-Wachtel pattern* (tall biphasic QRS in V3-V4)
    - If superior QRS axis (frontal plane): AV canal defect + VSD
        - LAD in perimembranous VSD: assoc. w/ membranous septal aneurysm
    - ↑ incidence of serious arrhythmias + SCD
    - Perimembranous VSD closure during cath: risk of RBBB, LAFB, & AVB

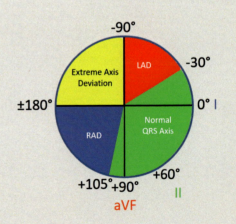

Patent Ductus Arteriosus

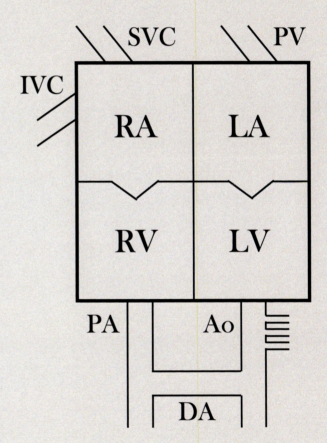

Key Points

Ductus arteriosus:
- Before birth: open vessel b/t PA & Ao
- After birth: closes & becomes ligamentum arteriosum

PDA: ductus arteriosus remains open after birth
- Associations: congenital Rubella syndrome
- Continuous "machine-like" murmur (Gibson's murmur)
- L-to-R shunt (acyanotic) → R-to-L shunt (differential cyanosis)

ECG features:
- Rhythm: NSR; ↑ incidence of IART & A-Fib w/ age
- PR interval: ↑ in 10-20%
- QRS axis (frontal plane): normal
- Small PDA: normal ECG
- Moderate-to-large PDA w/ significant L-to-R shunt: LAE ± LVH
    - LAE: prominent, wide terminal negative Pw in V1
    - LVH: deep S (V1) + tall R (V5-V6)
    - LBW infants: 22% LAE/LVH; 78% normal (low sensitivity)

Aortopulmonary Window

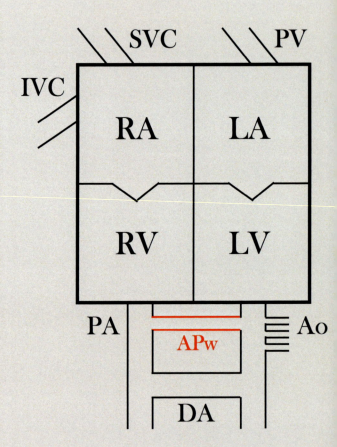

Key Points
- AP window: rare septal defect causing a connection b/t PA & Ao
  - Also known as AP septal defect or AP fenestration
  - Often isolated, but may occur with other CHDs
  - L-to-R shunt (acyanotic) → R-to-L shunt (cyanotic)
- ECG features: reflect hemodynamic abnormalities ("large PDA")
  - Small defect: normal ECG
  - Moderate-to-large defect: LAE ± LVH ± RVH
    - LAE: prominent, wide terminal negative Pw in V1
    - LVH: deep S (V1) + tall R (V5-V6)
    - RVH: tall R (V1) + deep S (V6); R:S ratio >1 (V1), <1 (V6)

Pulmonary Valve Stenosis

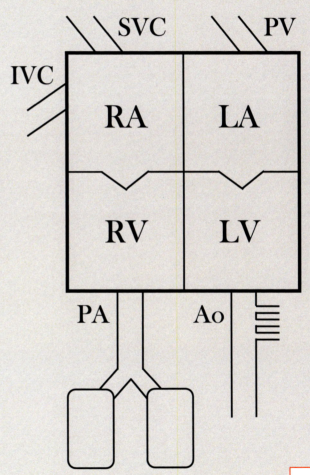

Key Points
- Congenial pulmonic stenosis: ↓ blood flow from RV to PA
  - Normal PV: 3 leaflets (2 leaflets = bicuspid PV)
  - Associations: tetralogy of Fallot, Noonan syndrome
  - MC than acquired form
  - Systolic ejection murmur (crescendo-decrescendo)
  - Critical stenosis: emergency; R-to-L shunt (cyanosis)
  - ECG useful in determining severity
- ECG features:
  - Mild stenosis: normal ECG or mild RAD (frontal plane)
  - Moderate stenosis:
    - RAD
    - V1: ↑ Rw amplitude ± rsR' pattern
  - Severe/critical stenosis:
    - Marked RAD
    - V1: monophasic Rw >20 mm (2 mV) ± rsR' pattern
    - RAE: ↑ Pw amplitude in II & initial positive Pw deflection in V1
    - RVH pattern (MC in adults)
    - Qw in V1-V3
  - Isolated pulmonic stenosis: Rw amplitude in V1 correlates w/ RVSP
    - RVSP (mmHg) = [Rw amplitude in V1] x [5]

Aortic Valve Stenosis

Key Points
- Congenial aortic stenosis: ↓ blood flow from LV to Ao
  - Normal AV: 3 leaflets (2 leaflets = bicuspid AV)
  - Less common than acquired form
  - Systolic ejection murmur (crescendo-decrescendo)
- ECG features:
  - ECG = poor predictor of severity
    - Normal ECG does not r/o severe AS
  - LV strain pattern: not helpful post-AVR (vs. MRI)
    - V1: ↑ Sw amplitude
    - V6: ↑ Rw amplitude
    - V5-V6: STD + TWI
  - ↑ Pw dispersion → ↑ risk A-Fib
  - ↑ QT interval dispersion ± SCD
    - Balloon valvuloplasty → ↓ QT dispersion

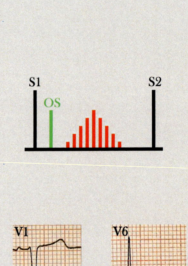
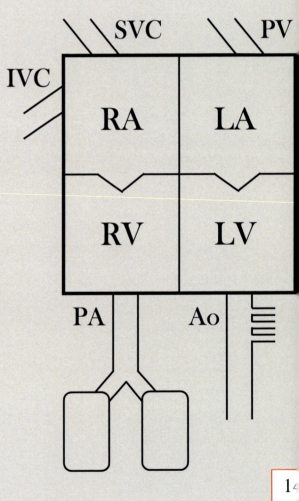

L-Transposition of the Great Arteries

Key Points

Great arteries = PA & Ao
TGA = [PA off LV] + [Ao off RV]
1. D-TGA: Ao ↔ PA; cyanotic; 2 circuits
2. L-TGA: LV/MV ↔ RV/TV; acyanotic; 1 circuit

L-TGA: ventricular inversion
- "Congenitally corrected TGA (CCTGA)"
- Associations: VSD; Ebstein-like malformation of systemic AV valve
- Maternal RFs: diabetes, Rubella, poor nutrition, alcoholism, >40 y/o

ECG features:
- R-to-L intraventricular septal activation (inversion of bundle branches): Qw in V1-V2
- 1st-, 2nd-, or 3rd-degree AVB
- Ventricular preexcitation w/ WPW syndrome or concealed accessory AV connections

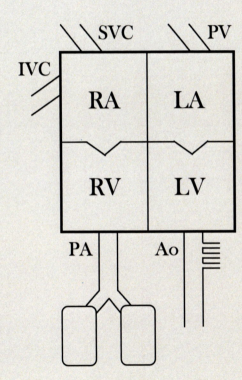
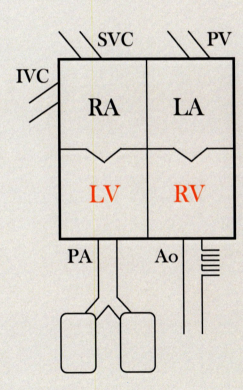

Anomalous Left Coronary Artery from the Pulmonary Artery (ALCAPA)

Key Points

- ALCAPA: LCA off PA
  - LCA normally off L-posterior aortic sinus
    - Also known as Bland-White-Garland syndrome
    - Coronary steal + $\downarrow O_2$ → coronary insufficiency
- ECG features:
  - Qw ≥3 mm deep & ≥30 ms wide in I, aVL, V5-V6 (esp. if absent in II, III, aVF)
  - MC in ALCAPA (vs. nonischemic CM):
    - Qw >30 ms wide in I
    - Qw >3 mm in aVL

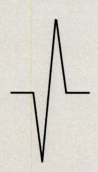

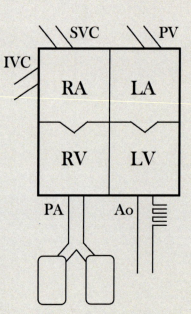

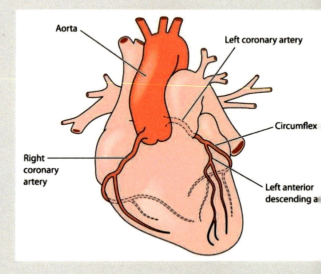

Anomalous Left or Right Coronary Artery from the Contralateral Sinus of Valsalva

Key Points

Aortic sinus (sinus of Valsalva) = anatomic dilatations of ascending aorta (just above aortic valve)
1. L-aortic sinus → LCA
2. R-aortic sinus → RCA
3. Posterior aortic sinus → none = noncoronary sinus

Anomalous coronary artery from contralateral aortic sinus
- ALCA = LCA off R-sinus of Valsalva
- ARCA = RCA off L-sinus of Valsalva
- Rare; ALCA > ARCA; often asymptomatic
- Associated with SCD (unknown mechanism)

ECG features:
- Often normal ± minor abnormalities before SCD
  - Ventricular ectopy or nonspecific-Tw changes

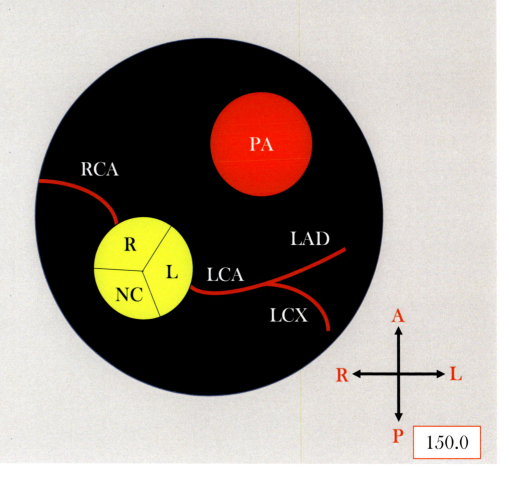

Left Ventricular Noncompaction

Key Points

- Normal: sponge-like (NC) → smooth & solid muscle fibers (C)
- LVNC: remains sponge-like (NC; "spongiform cardiomyopathy")
  - Cause: inherited (MC; gene mutations) or acquired
  - Isolated or associated w/ other CHDs or cardiomyopathies
  - Diagnosis via ECHO: ↓ LV function; NC/C ratio >2
    - ↑ ratio: ↑ trabecular thickness or ↓ compacted layer thickness
  - ↑ risk: heart failure, thromboembolic events, & fatal arrhythmias
- ECG features:
  - Biventricular hypertrophy (Katz-Wachtel pattern)
  - Sinus node & AV node abnormalities
  - Arrhythmias:
    - A-Fib → systemic arterial embolism → stroke, ischemia
    - V-Tach/V-Fib → SCD
  - WPW syndrome (+ tachycardia)

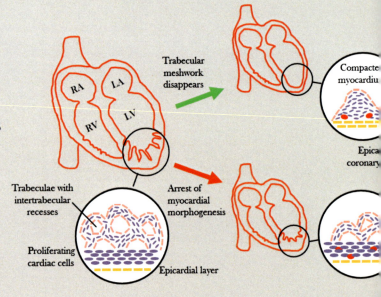

D-Transposition of the Great Arteries

Key Points

TGA = [PA off LV] + [Ao off RV]
1. L-TGA: LV/MV ↔ RV/TV; acyanotic; 1 circuit
2. D-TGA: Ao ↔ PA; cyanotic; 2 circuits; "complete TGA"
   - Associations: VSD
   - Maternal RFs: diabetes, Rubella, poor nutrition, alcoholism, >40 y/o

ECG features:
- Newborn infant: normal ECG for age
- If not repaired early: no RV regression
- If large VSD: biventricular hypertrophy
- Isolated LVH rare → suggests RV hypoplasia
- After Senning or Mustard procedure:
  - RVH + RAD ± RAE
  - Sinus node dysfunction; atrial tachyarrhythmias
  - Sudden death (ECG not predictive)
- After arterial switch procedure (Jatene switch):
  - Resolution of RV predominance
  - Follow-up: normal ECG (rest & exercise) & sinus node function; chronotropic incompetence not affecting working capacity in 1/3
  - If RV or LV predominance: may suggest anastomotic sites in great arteries

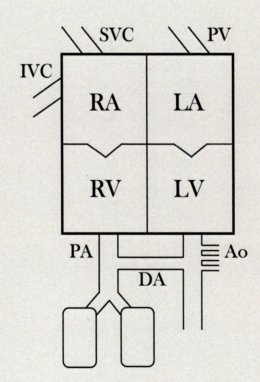
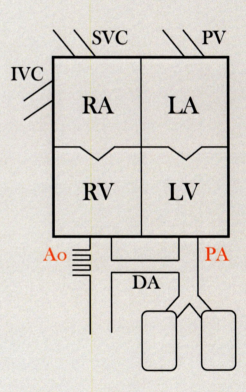

Tetralogy of Fallot

Key Points

- Tetralogy of Fallot (ToF): #1 cyanotic CHD
  - 4 characteristic features: (1) RVOT obstruction (pulmonic stenosis; determines severity); (2) RVH; (3) VSD (R-to-L shunt); (4) overriding aorta
  - Associations: R-aortic arch; collateral vessels supplying PA; coronary artery abnormalities; PDA; trisomy 21 (DS); DiGeorge & velocardiofacial syndromes
- ECG features:
  - RVH (hallmark; loss of normal RV regression) ± RAD ± RAE
    - If LAD: consider associated complete AV canal
    - QRS axis (frontal plane): normal or RAD; LAD (5-10%)
  - Post-surgical repair:
    - Atrial tachycardia & sinus node dysfunction (Pw duration dispersion)
    - Conduction defects: RBBB (common), LAFB
    - Assoc. w/ ↑ RVV:
      - QRS >150 ms &/or R-superior QRS axis (frontal plane)
      - If also PV insufficiency → consider PV replacement
    - QRST time integral values in precordial leads: correlated w/ ↑ RVV & RVP
    - QRS duration: directly correlated w/ RV volume & mass
    - ↑ QRS duration: assoc. w/ residual RVOT & PV insufficiency
      - Transannular patch repair: slows QRS widening
    - Predictors of ventricular arrhythmias (V-Tach) ± SCD:
      - QRS duration ≥180 ms (100% sensitivity, 96% specificity)
      - Abnormal QT & JT dispersion (pre- & post-op)
      - Ventricular late potentials (only post-op 2/2 scarring)
      - HR variability; LV size & dysfunction; microvolt Tw alternans

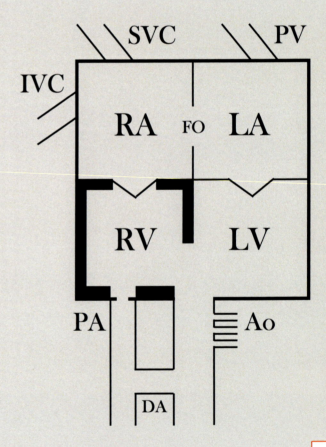

Truncus Arteriosus

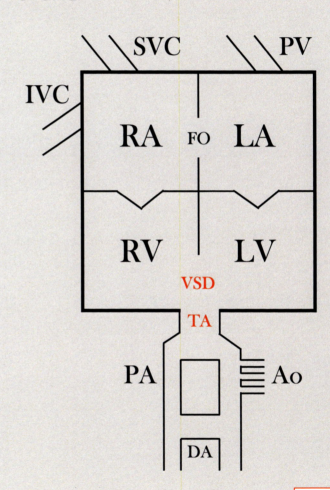

Key Points
Truncus arteriosus (TA; common arterial trunk): rare cyanotic CHD
- RFs: tobacco abuse, ↑ maternal age, 22q11.2 deletions (DiGeorge)
- Pathophysiology: common outflow tract from RV & LV 2/2 failure of conotruncal separation during embryogenesis
  o Depends on pulmonary circulation; 3 influencing factors: severity of (1) pulmonary vascular resistance, (2) truncal valvular insufficiency, & (3) aortic arch abnormalities
- Associations: VSD; abnormal aortic arch or coronary artery origin

ECG features:
- Newborn: normal or RVH
  o RVH: RAD, prominent Rw in V1-V3, R/S ratio <1 in V5-V6
- If persistent TA: depends on degree of pulmonary overcirculation
  o Significant pulmonary overcirculation → RVH + LVH + LAE
- Post-surgical repair:
  o ? ventricular arrhythmia ± SCD (? similar to ToF)

Pulmonary Atresia with Intact Ventricular Septum

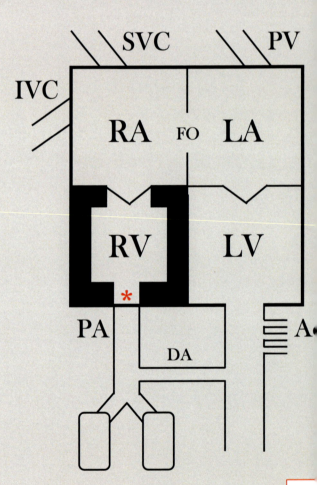

Key Points
- Pulmonary atresia: abnormal pulmonary valve development
  - Cyanotic CHD ("blue-baby syndrome"); requires surgical repair
  - Associations: VSD
- ECG features:
  - RAE: tall, peaked Pw in II &/or ↑ initial Pw amplitude in V1
    - Pw amplitude: correlates w/ degree of TR
    - Biatrial enlargement (rare)
  - QRS axis: leftward & inferiorly (frontal) + posteriorly (horizontal)
    - If normal/enlarge RV cavity: *rightward* & inferiorly (frontal) + *anteriorly* (horizontal)
  - ↓ RV potentials due to ↓ RV cavity, but hypertrophied RV wall

Ebstein's Anomaly

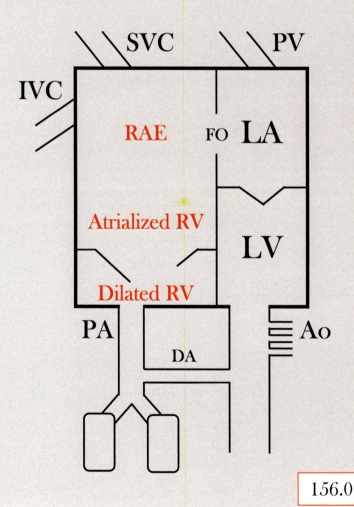

Key Points

Ebstein's anomaly: malformation of TV & RV
- Rare cyanotic CHD; ↑ incidence w/ maternal lithium use
- Pathophysiology: [incompetent, downward displaced TV] + [dilated & atrialized RV] → TR & ↓ forward flow
- Associations: interatrial connection (PFO, ASD); WPW; VSD; PDA; coarctation of the aorta; pulmonary outflow tract obstruction
- Presentation: depends on severity; consider age at presentation
  - Infant = HF; child = murmur; adolescent/adult = arrhythmia

ECG features:
- RAE: tall, peaked Pw (II, V1)
- WPW: [short PR interval] + [delta wave] + [↑ QRS duration]
  - Often R-sided accessory pathway (Kent bundle)
- Low-voltage, wide R' in R-precordial leads (atypical RBBB)
- Conduction defects: RBBB, 1st-degree AVB
- QRS axis (frontal plane): normal or LAD
- Rhythm: NSR, EAR, IART, A-Flut, A-Fib, AVRT, V-Tach, Mahaim-type preexcitation (normal PR + delta wave + ↑ QRS)

156.0

Tricuspid Atresia

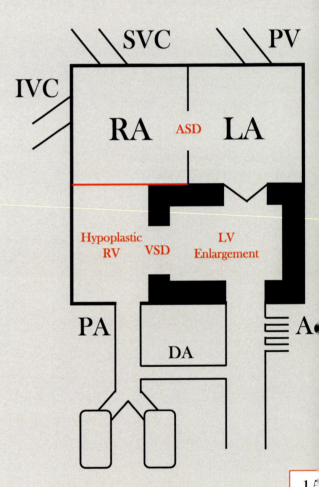

Key Points
- Tricuspid atresia: TV agenesis → no RA-RV communication; cyanotic CHD
  - Associated cardiac lesions: ASD + hypoplastic RV ± VSD ± PDA
  - Classification: based on orientation of great arteries
    - Type 1: normal orientation of great arteries; ± pulmonary stenosis
      - ↓ pulmonary blood flow (depends on VSD & PDA)
    - Type 2: TGA + VSD
  - Presentation: cyanosis (depends on pulmonary circulation; ↓ = sooner)
  - 3-stage surgery: (1) ↑ or ↓ pulmonary circulation (1st wks) → (2) SVC-PA connection (3-6 mos) → (3) IVC-PA connection (18-36 mos)
- ECG features:
  - Cyanosis + pathognomonic triad: (1) LAD, (2) LVH, (3) RAE (tall Pw)
  - Pw amplitude: poor correlation w/ intraatrial communication size & RAP
  - PR interval: short ("pseudo-preexcitation" > preexcitation) or prolonged
  - L-superior QRS axis (frontal plane) + cyanotic CHD → tricuspid atresia
  - LVH: deep Sw in R-precordial leads + tall Rw in L-precordial leads
  - ↓ RV potentials (hypoplastic RV; esp. in type 1)
  - QRS amplitude: poor correlation w/ VSD size & ventricular wall thickness
  - Post-Fontan: atrial arrhythmias, AVRT (WPW), AVNRT
  - Fetal ECG: accelerated ventricular rhythm

Hypoplastic Left Heart Syndrome

Key Points

HLHS: underdeveloped L-heart ± MV, AV, & Ao abnormalities
- Cyanotic CHD (M>F); unclear etiology; ductus dependent
- HLHS spectrum: depends on MV & AV lesion
- Presentation: depends on PDA & nonrestrictive ASD
- Management: PGE, ± atrial septoplasty, 3-staged surgery

ECG features:
- Newborns: may be normal
- RVH: qR pattern in R-precordial leads (V1, V34, V4R)
- Hypoplastic LV: ↓ Rw in L-precordial leads ± ↑ Sw in V6
- RAD & RAE: less common
- ST segment abnormalities (2/2 inadequate coronary perfusion)

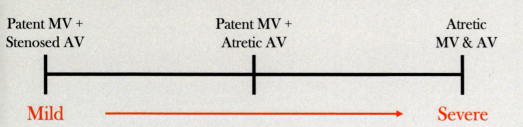

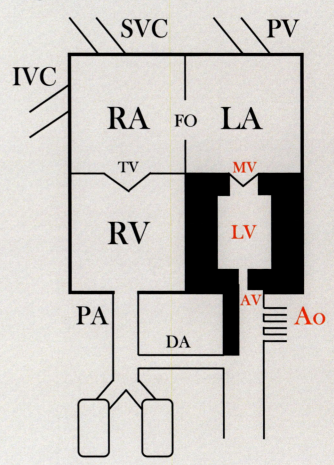

Single Ventricle Defects

Key Points
- Single ventricle defect = only 1 functioning ventricle
    - Examples: HSLS; pulmonary atresia w/ intact ventricular septum; tricuspid atresia; double outlet LV/RV
    - Presentation: depends on type & severity of defect
    - Treatment: staged reconstruction
- ECG features:
    - Biventricular hypertrophy: predominance depends on ventricular chamber morphology & orientation
    - Atrial enlargement: reflects AV valve stenosis/insufficiency or degree of ventricular dysfunction

HLHS
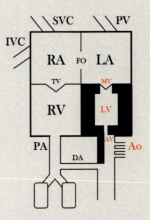

PA w/ Intact VS
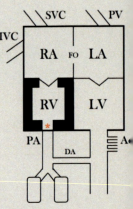

Tricuspid Atresia
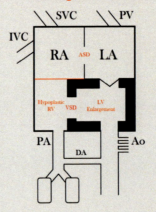

Double Outlet LV
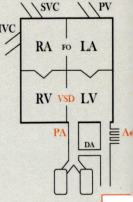

Fontan Palliation

Key Points

- Fontan palliation: univentricular hearts (tricuspid atresia, HLHS)
  - 3-staged reconstruction: excellent prognosis
    1. Norwood-Sano (1st few weeks): neoaorta + shunt
    2. Glenn (3-6 mos): remove shunt + **SVC to PA**
    3. Fontan (18-36 mos): **IVC to PA**
- ECG features: depends on underlying physiology
  - STD (likely 2/2 ventricular hypertrophy + strain)
  - Sinus node dysfunction (less common)
  - Tachyarrhythmias: V-Tach; atrial (↑ Pw duration & dispersion)

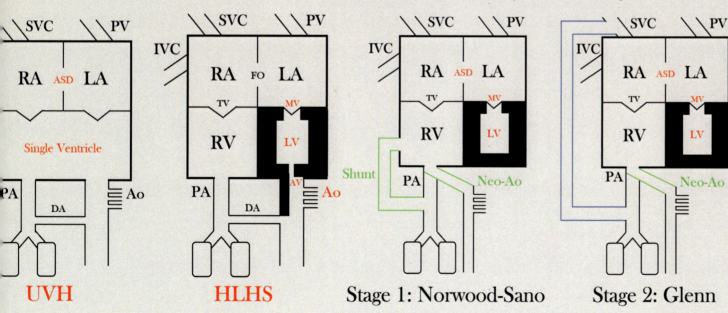